crafting gratitude

crafting gratitude

creating *and* celebrating our blessings *with* hands *and* heart

MAGGIE OMAN SHANNON

Published in the United States by Viva Editions, an imprint of Start Midnight, LLC, 101 Hudson Street, Thirty-Seventh Floor, Suite 3705, Jersey City, NJ 07302.

Printed in the United States.
Cover design: Scott Idleman/Blink
Cover photograph: iStock
Text design: Frank Wiedemann
Illustrations: Jill Turney
First Edition.
10 9 8 7 6 5 4 3 2 1

Trade paper ISBN: 978-1-63228-034-3
Ebook ISBN: 978-1-63228-039-8

Library of Congress Cataloging-in-Publication Data is available on file.

Gratefully dedicated to two special teachers who shaped my life:

To Lee Gaillard, who told me I was a writer when I was fifteen, giving me encouragement, aspiration, and an identity that continues to motivate me; and

To Ed Long, whose grounding in art, music, and film has enriched my life immeasurably and whose devotion to stoking the creative spirit inspires me still.

Table of Contents

"Gratitude unlocks the fullness of life. It turns what we have into enough, and more. It turns denial into acceptance, chaos into order, and confusion into clarity. It turns problems into gifts, failures into success, the unexpected into perfect timing, and mistakes into important events. Gratitude makes sense of our past, brings peace for today, and creates a vision for tomorrow."

—MELODY BEATTIE

"As I express my gratitude, I become more deeply aware of it. And the greater my awareness, the greater my need to express it. What happens here is a spiraling ascent, a process of growth in ever-expanding circles around a steady center."

—BROTHER DAVID STEINDL-RAST

"[Appreciation] makes immortal all that is best and most beautiful . . . . It exalts the beauty of that which is beautiful . . . . It strips the veil of familiarity from the world, and lays bare the naked and sleeping beauty, which is in the spirit of its forms."

—PERCY BYSSHE SHELLEY

Foreword

WE HUMAN BEINGS ARE CONTINUOUSLY LOOKING FOR WAYS to ease or avoid the painful parts of life. We are also created to create. So many of us waited and waited for the permission or the credentials to call ourselves creative when in fact we are each born creative. Not only is our creativity meant to be a great joy to us through all the days of our life, our creativity also is a part of our thriving survival. All of us are creative in our own ways and it is my firm belief that our creativity is also our best, most personalized medicine for what ails our individual hearts. Fortunately, our creativity is also very often the best medicine for what ails the hearts of others. What is life for if not to ease each other's burdens, to see the awe and wonder of life and to find our own way on our own creative paths?

For as long as I can remember, my first solution to my heartache or my boredom was to make something with my hands. When I learned the power of gratitude, my new go-to for emotional discomfort consisted of compiling a mental or handwritten list of all of the things in life for which I could be grateful. Combining these two practices is a powerful match.

I went through a very difficult decade where each day I was met with the challenge of not knowing whether or not I could continue on. My husband of 14 years sustained a traumatic brain injury and he became a completely different person. At this time, we had five young children and a business that we had built together. We had a farm to take care of and many obligations that had to go by the wayside so that I could care for my husband. As a caretaker, I had very little time to think about my own needs and over time, I deteriorated emotionally and physically.

It was gratitude and creativity that came to my rescue regularly. With my hands, I would have a conversation with God. I call my creative time my communing time. There are so many ways of prayer. Creativity is a way of prayer. The connection we have as we are creating is fertile soil for very personal communion, conversation, and insights that come through going into that zone of pure truth that comes as we are using our hands, our hearts, and our minds to know the next step to take in life. When we get into that zone, gratitude is inevitable and this changes our state of being. When we are grateful, we are healthier, stronger, and more receptive to everything good and true. We can heal. When we live in a state of grateful creativity through our own healing...we are led straight into helping others. Gratitude heals. Creativity heals. When we are healed, we can help. This is how we change the world.

It is with great enthusiasm that I highly endorse this beautiful manual of wisdom, love, and practical ideas. What a gift to the world this book is.

This is no ordinary how-to book. As you peruse the pages, it is my hope that you will feel inspired to quiet yourself enough to hear the calling of your own soul toward what is the best creative route for you to take to find yourself in a place of deep gratitude. We each need a daily practice to center us in gratitude. Inside of these pages you will find many ways to begin or continue your journey to gratitude through using your inborn gifts of creativity. I know you will enjoy and appreciate it as much as I have.

All the best to you, dear souls.

Melody Ross
Founder, Brave Living Media
Star, Idaho

Introduction

THOUGH THE IDEA OF MAKING A PRACTICE OF GRATITUDE has recently entered our cultural zeitgeist, thanks in large part to Sarah Ban Breathnach's 1995 book *Simple Abundance* and its exploration of gratitude journals (which inspired media mogul Oprah Winfrey to keep a gratitude journal, and, well, the rest is history), its importance as a practice actually dates back to ancient times. The Greek and Roman philosophers Epictetus and Marcus Aurelius counseled the practice of gratitude, and exhortations to be thankful are found in the sacred scriptures of every major world religion. Modern science, notably pioneered by Robert Emmons, has borne out the physiological benefits of counting our blessings. Gratitude can have a beneficial impact not only on our physical health, but also on our psychological well-being. So there are clear, time-tested reasons why making a practice of gratitude can benefit our minds, bodies, and spirits—but even if we know that, it is not always an automatic or easy thing to do.

I rediscovered this firsthand when I had an epiphany in the Quick Lane waiting room in Colma, California, while working on this book. Over the previous few months, I had found myself becoming increasingly irritable and anxious—a condition I now refer to as "BMS," which stands for Book-Making Syndrome—and feeling rather overwhelmed by all the elements of my to-do list. At the time I was working on this, these included being the mother of an eleven-year-old; being a caregiver for my mother, who had advanced Parkinson's disease and dementia; being the senior minister—and sole employee—of a San Francisco church; and writing books in my "free time." And on that particular day I was unexpectedly waiting for my left-front tire to be fixed, an inconvenient interruption to an already packed schedule that was not exactly welcome.

I thank God—literally—that I had enough presence of mind to grab a book on my way to the tire shop to pass the time while I waited. And not just any book—a book on gratitude, on how expressing gratitude can smooth out the corners of any day, any situation, every life. As I was turning its pages with increasing excitement, the irony of my situation made itself clear to me: Here I was, stressed out and internally bemoaning all the work I had yet to do on my book-to-be—a book on gratitude. This book, which you're about to read. Thankfully, the clouds of my stormy steel-gray tension parted wide enough for me to be able to see that I had been approaching things all wrong: ungratefully! With that realization, my mind began to pivot, and I started feeling grateful for everything: grateful that my car had made it without incident down the highway to the mechanic. Grateful that it was fixed within the hour. Grateful that rather than replacing two tires, they were able to patch just one, for a grand total of $39.95. Grateful to even have a car, grateful to live in San Francisco, grateful for my family, grateful to have a job I dearly love, and grateful for the opportunity to write books on subjects I'm passionate about. Grateful, grateful, grateful. So grateful!

I tell that story because I think it's something we all can relate to. We live in a fast-paced, demanding world and are constantly assaulted by advertising and other cultural messages that tell us we need *more*, we need *new*, we need *better*. Even if we are aware, as I was, of the importance of tapping into our gratitude, we can easily be seduced by society's siren calls of consumerism and envy and not-enough-ness. And even if we manage to stay free of that, we all live involved modern lives that are buzzing and busy, and are constantly overstimulated by technological intrusions that glut us with more data, more news, more ways to get off track. It's very hard to stay grateful in this kind of environment, which is why *Crafting Gratitude* is not only something that I think people need in general, but something that I also need myself. I need reminders to stay grateful; I need to remember, on a daily basis, the incredible, overflowing, abundant richness of my life. So this book is for both of us.

If you are artistically inclined, or even if you're not, it is my prayer that you will find at least one practice here—there are forty of them—that will resonate with you and prompt you to begin, or continue, exploring gratitude as a spiritual practice. As in the predecessor to this book, *Crafting Calm: Projects and Practices for Creativity and Contemplation*, you will find a potpourri of offerings, ideas, and inspiration for creating one or more gratitude practices using art and crafting materials as a medium. If you're new to this idea, you'll find suggestions for how to begin a gratitude practice ("Crafting a Gratitude Practice"), and a couple of real-life accounts of crafters explaining in their own words how an artistic endeavor became something more, something sacred ("Looking at Patterns"). And, as in *Crafting Calm*, you won't find a lot of detailed instructions for how to make these crafts. This is not so much a "how to" book, but a "why to" book; my intention here is to give you ideas for making these gratitude practices your own.

I believe that there is great spiritual power in using our hands to create expressions of the heart—especially when they're expressions of thankfulness. I believe this so strongly that I guess I take it for granted sometimes that everyone feels the same way. I got a very different message at a book signing for *Crafting Calm*, when a man in the audience came as close to heckling me as I've ever experienced. "*Why* did you write this book?" he kept asking me. Each time I would try approaching the answer in a different way, since he seemed to be searching for something that, clearly, I wasn't doing a good job of articulating. Finally, I answered from a place so deep that we both knew we had tapped a hidden wellspring of passion within me, and I am so grateful—yes, grateful!—that his repeated questioning helped me to find, finally, the words that express my feelings best. I wrote *Crafting Calm*—and the book you now hold, *Crafting Gratitude*—because I believe that every person is inherently creative. No matter what you think, no matter what you've been told, every person—and that includes you—is a creative person. And I know, from personal experience and from facilitating group workshops and retreats for almost two decades, that using art and craft materials as a form of meditation or prayer empowers people—helps them to connect with the Divine; helps them to see their own intrinsic creativity. And the reason I think that's so very, very important is that we live in this twenty-first-century world that is so complex and very often disheartening. We need empowered people. We need creative people. And without a doubt, we need the gifts and talents of all people to navigate the challenges that face us. That is why I have written these books—because we need *your* creativity, *your* gifts and talents. If you start with the creative and contemplative practices in this book, there's a real likelihood that you will want to employ your creativity in ever-widening arenas.

And the more I study gratitude and its wide-rippling effects, the more I become convinced that it is *the* key to life's riches—the most important practice that we as humans can undertake to improve the quality and to deepen the meaning of our lives. I feel that gratitude is the practice of a lifetime that we can keep unpeeling, layer by layer, going deeper and deeper until we truly understand what humanitarian Albert Schweitzer meant when he wrote these words: "The greatest thing is to give thanks for everything. He who has learned this knows what it means to live. He has penetrated the whole mystery of life: giving thanks for everything."

I hope that in some small but significant way, this book will spark new ideas for enfolding the practice of gratitude into your daily life; that it will serve as a guide for new ways, perhaps unexpected ways, that you can make the act of thanksgiving a cherished part of your regular routine. Above all, it is my deepest prayer that this book will inspire you to look at all the people, places, and things in your life for which *you* are profoundly grateful, which, I have discovered, is the salve for every sadness, the answer for every anxiety, the energy that will make every day extraordinary. May we all craft gratitude all the days of our lives.

Maggie Oman Shannon
San Francisco, California

Chapter 1

Gratitude for Family, Friends, and Significant Others

Chapter 1:

Gratitude for Family, Friends, and Significant Others

"Gratitude is the way the heart remembers—remembers kindnesses, cherished interactions with others, compassionate actions of strangers, surprise gifts, and everyday blessings. By remembering we honor and acknowledge the many ways in which who and what we are has been shaped by others, both living and dead."

—ROBERT EMMONS

PEOPLE, OTHER PEOPLE, ARE THE MOST POWERFUL SHAPERS of our lives; through them we learn, love, and are formed into who we are, whether by emulating the traits we admire or by rejecting those we don't. Our interactions with others range from the superficial (a smile at a fellow shopper in the grocery store) to the profound (comforting another who has just learned of a loved one's death), but always, in ways large and small, conscious and unconscious, we are affected by them.

In our twenty-first-century Western world, we don't always have systems in place for truly acknowledging to others how much they impact our lives; nor do we, as Mexican and other Latin cultures do, have a regular ceremony for recognizing loved ones who have passed away, such as we see in the annual Day of the Dead *ofrendas* that are created every November 2 to honor those who have made us who we are.

In this section you'll find ideas for changing that—ideas that will inspire you not only to reflect on those people who have had an impact on your life, but to create small offerings to give or keep that will remind you always of how you have been blessed by their presence in your life. Especially we should give thanks to those who nurtured us in dark times; as Albert Schweitzer so eloquently reminds us, "Sometimes our light goes out but is blown into flame by another human being. Each of us owes deepest thanks to those who have rekindled this inner light."

"In ordinary life we hardly realize that we receive a great deal more than we give, and that it is only with gratitude that life becomes rich."

—DIETRICH BONHOEFFER

Legacy Boxes

For creativity coach and women's group leader Judy Ranieri, gratitude has become a daily, even hourly, practice: "It totally changed my life once I became aware of gratitude at a very different level," she says. She remembers the events that led up to that awareness:

"About four or five years ago I went to Italy and thought that everything seemed so different there: sights, sounds, tastes, smells. When I came back home, the memories of the trip opened up this whole door of the senses, which developed into a gratitude practice of really being acutely aware of everything around me.

"Now I actually start my day out by going through my senses and giving gratitude for hearing the birds sing, the wind blow, smelling the bacon my neighbor is cooking—or just feeling my body sitting in a chair, or the comfort of my bed, seeing the sunlight starting to peek in."

For Judy, the people around her are also a focus of gratitude: "There's another thing that I do in the course of a day," Judy says, "that's become really important, and the more I do it, the more joy I experience: With every interaction, regardless of where or who it is, I make eye contact and smile to acknowledge people. It's a simple thing, but the reaction I get from it is incredible—it's a way to say 'I see you.' I go up to strangers now and compliment them."

Given Judy's tendency to "see" people, perhaps it's no surprise that one fundamental way she practices gratitude is by creating legacy boxes. The original concept for these boxes, Judy explains, was to make a "Grandmother's Wisdom box" for her grandchildren:

"I asked myself the question, 'What would I want my grandchildren to know about me if I were to die before they were born? How could I let them know what I valued, my life lessons, who I was as a person?' "

To answer that question for any future grandchildren, Judy started to fill a box with answers to those questions—and as she was starting this process, Judy found out that she would, in fact, soon have a granddaughter! "So the first thing I put into the box was a copy of the sonogram," Judy says, "and I wrote how it looked like the night sky and talked about the connectedness of all of us.

"I also wrote about the importance of keeping one's heart open—and found a mother-of-pearl heart that opened up, perfectly symbolizing that. Each item that I put into the box had a corresponding story around it: For example, a little figurine of Mickey Mouse as the Sorcerer symbolizes imagination and creativity—after all, he was just a rodent until Walt Disney used creativity and imagination to create his empire!"

And Judy continues to add to her box—poems; recipes; historical news clippings, such as one about Barack Obama's election as president of the United States; and more. She loves the concept and vehicle of the box so much that she started a small business selling boxes and offering workshops on how to make and use boxes for specific intentions and rituals.

She now guides people in making sweet-sixteen boxes, twenty-first birthday boxes, graduation boxes, and more: "I now have thirty-six different boxes that you can make," she says. People can make them for weddings, for Thanksgiving to place notes inside about what each individual member of the family is grateful for, for baby showers, to celebrate a brother or sister's birthday—there's a whole series of boxes that people can create!"

But as a gratitude practice, Judy recommends creating legacy boxes, which can be used to commemorate all kinds of different people in your life. "I love to make legacy boxes, because it's important for people to be acknowledged, recognized, validated. You can make them for favorite teachers, thanking them for what they've given you. And people of all ages can make one, including kids. For example, if you're making a legacy box for a teacher, kids can write thank-you notes to their teacher, or, if they're not writing yet, they can cut out pictures of how the teacher makes them feel.

"You could also use a box to do a family gratitude practice, where everyone writes down things to be grateful for over the course of one week and places them in the box, and then everyone can share their gratitudes at the end of that week.

"For me," Judy says, "the practice of gratitude lightens the load and refocuses me on just how much good there is in my life on a daily basis—and when I focus on that, the gratitude opens up doors by showing me how much good is in the world. I don't have to win a car to feel gratitude—it comes in very, very small ways and in gigantic ways. And the more I am aware of what I have to be grateful for, the more I appreciate it. It's the complete opposite of all the craziness that's going on in the world; it provides balance. Even when I start to get overwhelmed, I think: 'Am I okay right in this moment?' And that brings me back to gratitude. It's a form of grounding."

Inner Inquiries for Journaling and Reflection

- Who are the people who have left or are leaving a legacy for me—through their teaching, their example, their encouragement?
- Have I expressed my gratitude to these people for their "living legacies"?

DIY (Do It Yourself): Crafting a Legacy Box

First, Judy counsels, you want to come up with a theme: Who are you making this legacy box for, and what purpose do you want it to have? (See some examples above—is your legacy box celebrating a particular event or rite of passage, such as a wedding, birthday, or graduation, or is it simply to express love and appreciation to someone special in your life?) The next step is finding some kind of box. Judy says that shoe boxes are a good choice, though you can also buy boxes through her website and at art supply and craft stores. Then, cover the box with a collage of images symbolizing the occasion or person you're celebrating. For instance, if you're making a legacy box for a teacher, you could use images of pencils, notebooks, and other teaching supplies.

Once that's done, you can sit down and complete your legacy box all at one time, or you can work on it over a period of time, continuing to add items, images, or thoughts to the box as you have different experiences. What you place into the box is up to you; that teacher's box, for example, might include a strip of gold-star stickers, a box of the teacher's favorite fountain-pen ink cartridges, a package of dehydrated apple chips—anything that you feel symbolizes the regard you have for the recipient.

Crafting a Gratitude Practice

"If someone is just starting out and wants to craft a daily gratitude practice, I would suggest the waking-up exercise that I do—before getting out of bed, just start your day by going through all your senses, noticing what is affecting each one, and giving gratitude for those things. It really jump-starts my day. It used to be the to-do list that I focused on; now it's about gratitude. I find it to be very simple and powerful."

—JUDY RANIERI

"You are not obligated to thank God for your life, for your job, for your prosperity. However, giving thanks is an important state of your consciousness which keeps you in an awareness of oneness with divine flow. When you understand this you see that a grateful heart does not need something to be grateful for. One can be grateful with the same spontaneity as being happy. It simply flows forth from within and becomes a causative energy."

—ERIC BUTTERWORTH

Gratitude Beads

Prayer beads, for me, are both a polestar of avid study and an object of pure passion. Ever since 1998, when I asked twenty women friends to celebrate my fortieth birthday with me by bringing a bead (some brought two) to my party, and then later made myself a prayer-bead necklace from those beads, I have been captivated and nourished by the practice. In the years since, I have strung prayer beads for different concerns, representing my child, my marriage, my business, my pet; as well as two prayer-bead shawls that I wore at each of my ordinations: as an interfaith minister (using colorful beads and charms representing all faith traditions) in 2010, and as a Unity minister (using iridescent white and crystal beads and silver charms with Unity symbols) in 2014. I even cowrote a book about prayer beads in 2003, titled *A String and a Prayer: How to Make and Use Prayer Beads.*

So you might say I know something about this wonderful practice. But there's one thing I hadn't done before, and that was to actually make the beads themselves!

In her self-published book *The Threaded Gem Adventure: or How to Connect the Jewels in Your Life*, author Malana Ashlie explains her practice of "crafting relationships through beads." As I did to celebrate my fortieth birthday, Malana—who lives in Honduras—asked her friends around the world to send her a bead (new or from a piece of their own jewelry) for her sixty-fifth birthday. Because she was living in a distant land and deeply missed her friends and family members, she wanted to use these offerings to create a necklace that would embody the spirit of everyone dear to her. If a cherished friend or family member had passed away, she asked one of their loved ones to select a bead and place it on top of something that had belonged to the deceased person so that it could absorb his or her energy. It proved to be a very spiritual experience for her—one she calls a "journey of awareness"—and gratitude was part of her process, especially each time she received a new bead.

But Malana goes one step further in her book; she suggests actually making beads out of paper, writing special messages on the paper strips before rolling them up to seal and paint as beads—a message bead, if you will, on which you can write messages (like "I love you"), prayers (like "God bless you"), or wishes (like "Be happy").

And this wonderful suggestion prompted within me an idea for a gratitude practice: What if we listed all our gratitudes on these strips of paper, then made the beads to string on a gratitude necklace—the beads of which could literally be used to count one's blessings? Or what if we created a bead to represent each person who has touched our life, for whom we're grateful? Malana counsels that these paper beads are not the most durable, but with all the gifts of life, and people in life, that come to us through the days, we can always create new gratitude beads!

Inner Inquiries for Journaling and Reflection

- Who are the people I'm grateful for on the "string" of my life? How can I remember or connect with them more frequently?
- What are the gratitudes and blessings that I want to remember on a daily basis? What is it that I enjoy but sometimes take for granted?

DIY: Crafting Gratitude Beads

On a sheet of plain white 8½" by 11" paper, make marks with a pencil at ½-inch intervals along each short edge. Then, place a ruler on a slight diagonal from the corner on one edge to the first dot on the other edge. Cut along the ruler with an X-ACTO knife, as that will make the cleanest cut. You will have a long, narrow, triangular piece of paper. Repeat, placing the ruler and cutting, until the entire sheet is cut into equal-sized triangular strips.

Then, using a fine-line marker, write one of your blessings, something you are grateful for, on each strip. Color the opposite side; this will be the outside of the bead.

Starting at the widest end, begin to roll a strip of paper around a round wooden toothpick, keeping the paper pulled straight and taut. Once the entire strip is rolled up, put a touch of white glue on the end portions and set the bead, still on the toothpick, aside to dry. Repeat until you've used all the paper strips.

Once the glue is dry, paint each bead with a sealer, being careful not to let the sealer touch the wooden toothpick. (You can also use clear nail polish.)

When the sealer is dry to the touch, spin the bead gently to loosen it from the toothpick. Apply a second coat of the sealer and dry. Repeat for two to three more coats. When the final coat is dry, you will have a set of gratitude beads to string!

> "Gratefulness is the key to a happy life that we hold in our hands, because if we are not grateful, then no matter how much we have we will not be happy, because we will always want to have something else or something more."
>
> —BROTHER DAVID STEINDL-RAST

New Life Baby Blankets

For Aida Merriweather, an interfaith minister, knitting has been a part of life since she learned how to knit at the age of six in a French school, where it was part of the curriculum. Through the years, she also has found it to be a powerful spiritual practice. Aida started by making prayer scarves, then prayer shawls, after reading the book *Knitting into the Mystery*. Now she makes baby blankets in gratitude for new life.

For her, making a baby blanket to honor new life has been a powerful practice: "I mostly make them for parishioners when I discover there will be a new addition to their family," she says. "If I know the baby's name, I sing or say it as I'm knitting. I love the idea of wrapping little ones in warmth and love. Because I have been making them for a while, I have some fun stories to tell: I made one for someone who's now a senior in college, and she still has it!"

Aida has found gratitude to be a heart-opening process: "Paying attention to and appreciating what I have in my life, and what others bring to my life—it opens my heart. Even if someone just opens the door for me or welcomes me into a building, I find my heart opening. In this world that has so many challenges, that kind of kindness and care makes me look at what I have instead of what I don't have.

"Gratitude has been a practice that inspires me and strengthens me, deepens me to live more fully, to take more risks, to appreciate what a gift my life is, and to review even in the moment—'Wow, that was really nice.' It helps me be present."

Aida remembers a recent recipient of one of her New Life Baby Blankets: "I just delivered a baby blanket to a pregnant nurse who helped me when I had to have some medical treatments; her presence was so calming. I was so grateful for and impressed by her kindness that I made her a baby blanket. I made one with autumn colors since she was due in October. I gave it to her and told her that I wanted to honor her new beginning, since she helped me with my new beginning."

Aida also makes "waiting" blankets for people who are going to adopt, and she enjoys picking a color of yarn that she thinks the recipients will resonate with. "There's that joy in new life, new arrivals, new beginnings," Aida says. "Honoring those is the kind of thing that really helps me and helps others. There's a kind of reciprocity there that shows me how I can contribute and give something back in a meaningful way.

"I worked in a children's library for a long time, so that's another reason why the idea of new life and new beginnings means so much to me," Aida adds. "One of my favorite baby blankets was one I gave to someone whose daughter was named Aurora. I thought it was a hoot that, just like in the fairy tale, Merriweather [Aida's last name] was making a blanket for Aurora!

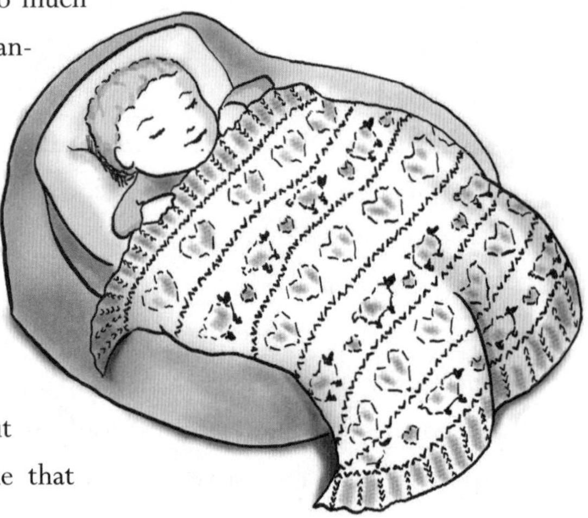

"And I recently made one for the granddaughter of a parish administrator; there was something about this woman's excitement about meeting her granddaughter for the first time that really touched me. I chose colors of variegated purple, and I heard that it's the baby's favorite blanket—and when I saw a photograph of her, so sweet in her purple blanket, then I could see it: new beginnings!"

Inner Inquiries for Journaling and Reflection

- What signs of new life are in *my* life right now? What is being born in me . . . and around me?
- How could I honor this new life, whether it's literal or figurative? How can I show gratitude for the newness that is internally or externally being made manifest?

Crafting a Gratitude Practice

"When you're first starting out with a gratitude practice, it really depends on the person what might be helpful. One thing could be to pay attention to where you feel in your body that something is a nice surprise.

"Another practice is the one that Angeles [Arrien] suggested—to spend time reflecting on your day using these three questions from Spinoza: *What surprised you? What touched you? What inspired you?* Because sometimes asking 'For what am I grateful today?' doesn't quite do it. But asking what inspired you, well, I think inspiration is really close to gratitude, as is being touched by something. Start there."

—AIDA MERRIWEATHER

Thanksgiving Cards

Though sending thank-you notes is a time-honored and appropriate habit to cultivate, many people have lost the art of the thank you, preferring instead a quick e-mail—if any written thanks are given at all.

Perhaps *Tonight Show* host Jimmy Fallon can correct our cultural bad manners through his frequent comedy bit of writing thank-you notes, accompanied by a cloying keyboard refrain as he starts each one. Recipients of his past gratitude have included oatmeal ("thank you . . . for looking like I already ate you before I eat you"), email ("thank you, emails that say 'You have successfully unsubscribed from these emails,' for completely missing the point"), and people who make premature Thanksgiving plans ("thank you, people who are already making Thanksgiving plans . . . for helping people like me come up with early excuses to get out of those plans").

Whatever Jimmy Fallon may think about certain people's Thanksgiving plans, there's a Thanksgiving ritual that is a lovely practice to undertake in lieu of holiday cards: sending a Thanksgiving (or gratitude) card. I first heard of this practice from a friend, who even before the gratitude-journal craze of the early '90s made a point of sending heartfelt messages to the cherished people in his life every Thanksgiving, telling them exactly why they meant so much to him. And since then, I have learned that titans such as the late businessman and philanthropist Sir John Marks Templeton had this practice. Templeton once noted that "For more than thirty years, my family has sent Thanksgiving cards rather than Christmas cards to our friends, desiring to spread our gratitude for the many gifts of life."

Although my friend and Sir John chose to write to the people closest to them, you could expand this practice by giving Thanksgiving cards to others in your life who impact it in small but significant ways: your Starbucks barista, who makes your daily morning latte exactly like you want it; your mail carrier, who always makes sure to leave your packages under your gate, rather than inconveniently taking them back to the postal station for you to pick up the next day; or the administrative assistant in the front office of your child's school, who always answers questions efficiently and kindly.

Should you be artistically inclined (or even if you're not), crafting a card yourself would be especially appreciated. You can buy packages of ready-made blank notecards and envelopes at craft stores, and can personalize them with stickers, a "Thanks so much!" written in glitter glue, or a rubber-stamp design. What's most important here is taking the time to express your gratitude to the people who contribute to your life in large and small ways—and even though Jimmy Fallon's thank-you cards are spoofs, it doesn't hurt to review your blessings, from oatmeal to the people inviting you to Thanksgiving dinner!

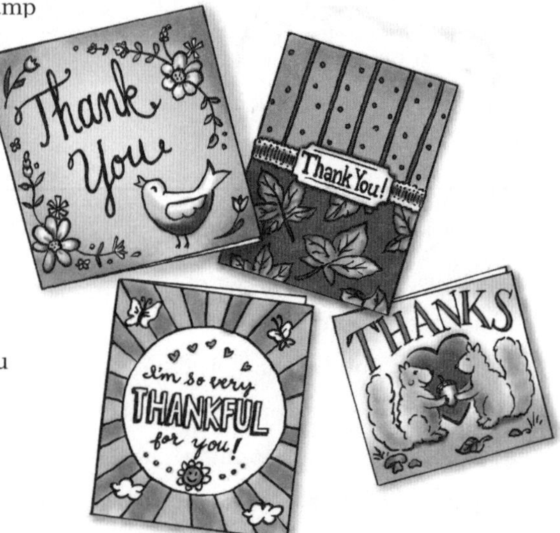

Inner Inquiries for Journaling and Reflection

- Who are the people who contribute to my life in significant ways—friends, family members, coworkers? Have I taken the time lately to thank them and tell them what they mean to me?
- Who are the people who make my life easier in small ways, who provide service with consideration and thoughtfulness? Have I let them know that they impact me in a positive way that I'm grateful for?

"Another reason we turn logical with our gratitude is that it is terrifying. The wonder of a moment in which there is nothing but an upwelling of simple happiness is utterly awesome. Gratitude is so close to the bone of life, pure and true, that it instantly stops the rational mind, and all its planning and plotting. That kind of let go is fiercely threatening. I mean, where might such gratitude end?"

—REGINA SARA RYAN

BLESSINGS IN A BASKET

I sift through the small basket made of golden wire into which I have placed sixty-five strips of lavender, pale green, and sky-blue paper. This was a present for my mother's sixty-fifth birthday, and on each strip I wrote a gratitude—something that I was grateful to my mother for.

As I look into this container, these Blessings in a Basket speak to me of memories that are growing mistier with time. As I write this, my mother is still alive, but the essence of who she was—is—has largely been scraped away through the malignant twins attending her now: advanced Parkinson's disease and dementia. It is sometimes hard to remember the person I celebrated through these paper strips, since the ravages of her disease have reduced our communication primarily to touch—a kiss on the forehead, a stroke on the forearm, a held hand.

Now this gift means as much to me as it might have meant to her, because I can see my mother again through my own words on each slip, each one holding a different gratitude: "8. I love you because you made every Christmas special when I was growing up." "55. I love you for how you can still get silly and love to laugh." "27. I love your openness to new ideas." "16. I love you for the courage you demonstrated when Daddy was dying."

I am so grateful that I was able to express gratitude to my mother in this way when she was still able to receive it—she held on to this basket and all the slips inside, and now it has become a gift to both of us. I did a similar thing when my relationship with my now-husband first deepened, though I used a small notebook instead of slips in a basket to catalog the things I loved and admired about him.

Whether you use a notebook, a box, or a basket to acknowledge your gratefulness for a special person in your life, it is worth the time and effort to do so. We never know how long we might have that person in our lives, or in what capacity, so it truly is a practice that is better undertaken sooner rather than later. As we do this—listing everything we can think of to be grateful for in this association, from the sublime ("39. I love you for the sacrifices you made for me while I was growing up") to the ridiculous ("36. I love the fact that you watch *Melrose Place*")—we come to know the words of Jean Baptiste Massieu in a very deep way: truly, "Gratitude is the memory of the heart."

Inner Inquiries for Journaling and Reflection

- Have I ever tried listing *all* the reasons that I love and appreciate a special person in my life?
- If I were to receive a gift of Blessings in a Basket, what would I want someone to have listed about me? What would I like someone to remember about me?

Chapter 2

Gratitude for Health

Chapter 2:

Gratitude for Health

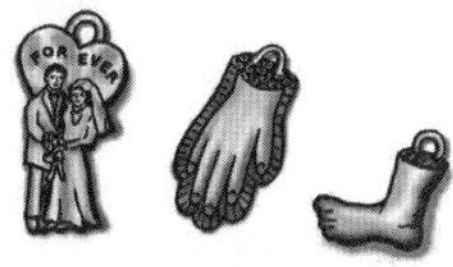

"Gratitude is a vaccine, an antitoxin, and an antiseptic."

—JOHN HENRY JOWETT

IN SOME WAYS, OUR BODIES CAN BE COMPARED TO CARS—they are the vehicles that we use to navigate our little corners of the world. And as with cars, sometimes we don't fully appreciate our bodies until they break down, until we're hit with an accident or disease that points out all too painfully what a gift we have when everything is functioning smoothly.

And it turns out that there are real reasons why we should count our blessings when we're faced with a health challenge—because according to scientific research, having a regular practice of gratitude can help us to sleep better, experience less stress, build our immune function, and exercise more. As Sharon Huffman, founder of the Center for

Enlightened Leadership, reminds us, "Feelings of gratitude release positive endorphins throughout the body, creating health."

In this section, you'll read stories of people who became more grateful for their ability to craft after an injury or illness, and you'll also get ideas for using a gratitude practice as a powerful healing tool while you're grappling with a health challenge. And should you ever find yourself in need of a gratitude practice when you're without art or craft supplies, there's none better than the one suggested by mind/body expert and author Joan Borysenko: "Thank God for what doesn't need healing."

"I see the practice of gratitude as a way of keeping the heart open, but also a way of retaining our humanity in a growing world of neck-and-neck darkness and light, or evolutionary and de-evolutionary forces in a race here. But I'm forever grateful for the great gift of life itself, and also just seeing all the evolutionary possibilities that we have ahead of us."

—ANGELES ARRIEN

HEALING HAIKUS

Marjorie Miles did not consider herself a writer, as she recounts in the introduction to her book, *Healing Haikus.* But her Muse had other ideas, and she announced her arrival in an unlikely place: the waiting room of Marjorie's oncological radiologist. As Marjorie writes, "While waiting in my radiologist's office, I began daydreaming. In that gauzy, gossamer state of consciousness between waking and sleeping, I heard the Voice. Simply and clearly, it said: 'You need to write a poem.' 'You've got to be kidding. *This* doesn't feel very poetic!' I snapped back. Ignoring me, the Voice continued, 'And the poem should be a *haiku!'*

"'A *what*? I am *not* a poet,' I grumbled. Yet, I began writing . . . and the haiku formula—five syllables in the first line, seven syllables in the second line, and five syllables in the last line—found its way to the scrap of paper I had been holding. Something powerful, mysterious, and incomprehensible had just occurred. When my oncology radiologist opened the door and entered the room, he startled me back to full consciousness. He had been detained at a meeting and apologized for arriving late to our appointment. Although I knew he was pressed for time, I felt compelled to tell him, 'I just wrote a poem . . . about radiation . . . and I would love to read it to you.'"

And so began Marjorie's foray into writing haiku as a form of gratitude practice—even in the midst of the most serious health challenge she had ever faced: lung cancer. She began to write haiku daily, and she found within the process that not only could she identify elements in her life to be grateful for, but indeed that crafting these tiny daily poems was helping her to heal. Her first haiku, the one she read to the doctor, reflected her gratitude for the medical treatment she was receiving:

Radiation . . . Zap!
Search and find the mutant cells
Glowing . . . going . . . GONE

And she continued to list things she was grateful for throughout the course of her chemotherapy treatment:

Thoughtful Volunteers
Bring compassion . . . pillows . . . food
Everyone is kind

What Marjorie discovered in her healing journey, which she detailed in her book, is that "there is something in each of us that is luminous and magical and remains untouched by disease. It is transcendent—and poetry is its voice. To hear that voice is to know what healing means. It is a return to wholeness."

Crafting gratitude through her daily haiku practice changed Marjorie's life in more ways than one. What a great prescription it is, as one of Marjorie's haiku wisely counsels us, to.

Savor the small joys
Daily gratitude focus
Creates deep meaning

Inner Inquiries for Journaling and Reflection:

- Am I giving daily gratitude for my health?
- If I am currently having a health challenge, what *can* I give thanks for?

> "I am grateful for my family and friends,
> a job to earn my keep, and the health to do it,
> and opportunities and the lessons I've learned.
> Let me never lose sight of the simple blessings
> that form the fabric and foundation of my life.
> I am blessed, yesterday, today, and tomorrow."
>
> —ABBY WILLOWROOT

Mojo Hands

They look like beautiful colored leaves from a distance, but if you look closely you will see that they are hands made of fabric, embellished with words and shapes created from beads and embroidery. These individual cloth hands—emerald green, slate blue, soft black—hung palm side up, with fingers trailing downward like fringe, look like *hamsa* hands: the hand-shaped amulets found in the Middle East and North Africa that serve as good-luck charms and protective talismans. And as in Jewish culture, which holds that the five fingers of the *hamsa* hand are to remind its wearer to use their five senses to praise God, so too are these Mojo Hands made as a gratitude practice.

Artist Søren Mason Temple has been making Mojo Hands in many different colors, with many different messages, for years now. Her favorite is one that has "Art Heals" embroidered on it in different shades of thread; its main focal point is a large beaded eye in the center of the hand. Søren explains:

"I can say 'Art Heals' because I know it to be true. I was miserable, lonely, and bullied in elementary school, but when I was making something I forgot all of that and focused only on what was forming out of my hands and imagination. I didn't remember how alone and afraid I was, and when I was done I had brought something new into the world. I could create happiness.

"Throughout my life I have had several debilitating illnesses that kept me close to home and unable to do a lot of what other people can do, but art is always there for me.

It is the part of me that isn't sick and the part of me that functions when the rest of me doesn't. It can be a place that's safe when everything else hurts.

"Sewing is my form of meditation and prayer—the calming, repetitive stitching and beading is done with focus and intention and it centers me and calms my wild mind.

"Every time someone tells me that my art means something to them, my aloneness is healed by that connection. By bringing beauty and meaning to life, making art makes me feel alive when nothing else does. When the world I am living in isn't where I want to be, I can create a new one and discover ways to bring those worlds together."

Søren explains that she began to create her Mojo Hands several years ago: "True mojo hands are a type of folk-magic practice that Wikipedia calls a 'prayer in a bag.' My version is a literal one with a 'prayer in a hand.' Their shape is a *hamsa* hand, a traditional Middle Eastern symbol of protection against the evil eye. Hands show up over and over in my artwork. For me, that symbol is about the power of physical creation to change and heal lives.

"I've spent years trying to train myself to focus on things I am grateful for, and it hasn't been easy—I was raised in a family who can see the worst in any situation.

"I go in and out of making gratitude lists, but I wanted something more tangible than writing, and something with extra focus.

"I hang the Mojo Hands on my walls so I am surrounded by these reminders all the time, and I have given them to people I love to let them know ways I am grateful for them."

Given the myriad ways in which hands convey our emotions and help us to relate to others, crafting a Mojo Hand to express your gratitude has many exciting possibilities indeed—too many, perhaps, to count on one hand!

Inner Inquiries for Journaling and Reflection

- What do hands mean to me—my own hands, my beloved's hands, my parents' hands, my child's or grandchild's hands?
- Do I give gratitude for the gifts, both tangible and intangible, that come through hands?

DIY: Crafting a Mojo Hand

Making a Mojo Hand can be a celebration of your own hands or of someone else's—this can be a great craft to do with a child! Trace the outline of each of your two hands on a piece of light-colored felt. Cut them out and embellish them on one side with beads, sequins, charms, or embroidery. As Søren does, you can write a special motto or gratitude reminder on your felt hands. When you're finished embellishing, stitch your two felt hands together on a sewing machine or with embroidery thread; you can even stuff them with batting if you like. Close the top of the "palm" last, perhaps affixing a loop to hang it with before closing it up. Depending on its size, you can hang it up or wear it. May it bring you good mojo!

Should you desire to emulate Soren's process for creating a more involved Mojo Hand, here are her instructions: "I created a pattern, because I wanted to make a series that would all be the same, but you could also draw freehand. Pin a piece of quilting cotton to a piece of felt and draw the shape you want. Machine stitch around the shape. Then embroider, bead, and sew your gratitude into the piece.

"I always end by beading one row on top of the machine-stitched shape for extra protection, and put a beaded loop for hanging them at the top of that. Cut around the outer edges with pinking shears."

"In moments of darkness and uncertainty, we encounter the depths of our desire that life go on. And, paradoxically, it opens us up to gratitude for this moment—our chance to breathe the air, feel our heart beating, look into the eyes of another being. In times like that, what's trivial or tawdry gets stripped away. And the stark grandeur appears. A grandeur that reaches down into our hearts."

—JOANNA MACY

The Meaning of Colors

Following is a list of colors and some qualities that are commonly associated with them. These associations may be helpful to you if you have a particular intention for your craft that you want to support with color.

RED: Confidence, courage, vitality

PINK: Love, beauty

ORANGE: Vitality with endurance

YELLOW: Happiness, intellectual energy

GREEN: Life, fertility, well-being

BLUE: Truth, peace

PURPLE: Spirituality, royalty

INDIGO: Intuition, meditation

BROWN: Earth, order

GOLD: Prosperity, wisdom

WHITE: Purity, cleansing

GRAY: Maturity, security

BLACK: Stability, mystery

"Happiness cannot be traveled to, owned, earned, worn or consumed. Happiness is a spiritual experience of living every minute with love, grace, and gratitude."

—DENIS WAITLEY

Looking at Patterns

"Two years ago, I took a nasty fall on the sidewalk when my foot got trapped in a broken drain. I broke my right hand, sprained my wrist, and tore the rotator cuff in my right shoulder. I was unable to use my arm at all for some time, and then had very limited use of my hand for many weeks. It was first in a cast, and then a series of immobilizing splints, and required months of physical therapy to regain mobility.

"I've been a crafter all my life, starting with making doll clothes, toy animals, and holiday decorations as a very young girl. I crochet, embroider, sew, scrapbook, and indulge in many more crafts than I could possibly list. But when I became a business owner twenty-plus years ago, I began to craft less and less. The business took so much of my time and creative energy that there rarely seemed to be enough left over to devote to crafts.

"Then came the accident, and suddenly, I literally *couldn't* craft. I was unable to hold a needle or hook, use scissors, or grip my crafting tools. It made me realize what an important part of my life crafting truly was. When the doctors warned me that my hand might not make a full recovery, I looked around at my crafting supplies, and felt as if the world was ending.

"I redoubled my efforts at physical therapy, and gradually became able to hold onto fat objects. I felt so grateful! The first thing I did was to run out and buy a size Q crochet hook, a giant hook more than 2 inches around. Using this hook to crochet a scarf became an essential part of my physical-therapy regimen.

"Over time, my hand has recovered about 85 percent. But my crafting has recovered about 1,000 percent! I now belong to four different groups who get together to craft. I work on craft projects while on trains and planes, in waiting rooms and meetings, while socializing and watching TV. My home office looks more like a crafting room than it does an office these days. Crafting has once again become a regular, essential part of my life.

"Every time I take out a craft project to work on, I experience a moment of gratitude that this is still something I can do. Having full use of my hands is such a precious gift! I plan to keep making the most of it for as long as I can."

—C. J. HAYDEN

Medicine Wheels

It was a clear, bright desert morning when I first discovered the powerful ritual of the medicine wheel. I was attending a modern-day Wisdom School, an in-depth learning intensive on the esoteric teachings of spiritual traditions across cultures, and I found myself one morning standing in a barren, scrubby landscape into which a large circle of stones had been placed. A Native American teacher led us through the ritual, and my experience of the medicine wheel engaged almost all of my senses—the sense of sight, as the bright-orange disc of sun ascended from the horizon; the sense of sound, as the teacher chanted in resonant waves; the sense of smell, slapped awake by the smoky tang of sage; the sense of touch, as I held a pouch of tobacco, my ceremonial offering, in my hands.

The building of a medicine wheel is a time-honored Native American tradition that uses the earth as its altar cloth, onto which is placed a ceremonial circle of stones. The circle pays homage to the four directions contained within it; its shape illustrates the interrelatedness of all things. Each direction on the medicine wheel is associated with a season, a time of day (and phase of human life), a totem animal, and a color.

By acknowledging and meditating on the elements of a medicine wheel, we honor and give gratitude to Spirit—the Source of all blessings in our lives. The medicine wheel is used for prayer, meditation, and spiritual rituals; it is also a tool of healing and a visual reminder of higher principles. But you don't have to be in a desert or even outdoors to work with the potent symbols of a medicine wheel—you can make a Medicine Wheel in your own bedroom or living room.

Inner Inquiries for Journaling and Reflection

- What "season" of my life am I in right now? What blessings are present in this time of life?
- Am I staying present to the interrelatedness of all things in life? How can I become more present to the fact that I am a part of all Creation, and all Creation is a part of me?

DIY: Crafting a Medicine Wheel

To begin this gratitude practice, decide if you want to make a two-dimensional medicine wheel or a three-dimensional one. If you simply want to work with paper, you can start by drawing a circle—then drawing or collaging the elements you want to place in each quadrant. If you incorporate this into a gratitude journal, you could use this drawing/collage as a focal point for expressing your thanks to the Divine.

Working three-dimensionally, you could create a Medicine Wheel altar. Using a dresser top or tabletop as your base, you can cover it with a special cloth and place small stones in a circular pattern. Refer to the box on page 40 or do your own research into what the four directions of a Medicine Wheel represent, and add a representation of those elements into each quadrant of your altar Medicine Wheel. (Be sure to use a real or online compass to note where the directions of your Medicine Wheel should lie.) By doing this, you are creating a sacred space, one that can shift and change with time, in which to meditate on the blessings of life and give thanks.

Associations and Symbols to Work With in a Medicine Wheel

Below are some common symbols associated with the directions in a medicine wheel. Please note that this is a general reference for common associations; these might differ in particular indigenous traditions.

THE EAST is the direction for seeking illumination or clarity about your life path. Its associations and symbols include the dawn or sunrise, spring, new beginnings, seedlings, innocence, play, childhood, and the Sun or Earth. Its elements are air or fire; its colors are yellow, orange, and green, and its totem animal is the eagle.

THE SOUTH is the direction of humility, faith, and trust. Its associations and symbols include midday, summer, adolescence, the physical body, passion, harvest, abundance, and ripeness. Its element is earth or fire; its colors are red, orange, and yellow; and its totem animals are the mouse and coyote.

THE WEST represents introspection, going within to hibernate (as its totem animal does) and review your desires and goals. Its associations and symbols include dusk or sunset, adulthood, autumn, leaves dropping, letting go, surrendering with faith and trust, the Moon, the unconscious, healing, and dreams. Its element is water, its colors are black and blue, and its totem animal is the bear.

THE NORTH represents wisdom, gratitude, and giving thanks for blessings. Its associations and symbols include midnight, old age, winter, frozen landscapes, silence, communion with Spirit, intuition, grounding, and being filled with the Divine. Its element is air or wind, its color is white, and its totem animal is the buffalo.

THE CENTER represents the integration of all; it is timeless, ageless, and pure openness in the present moment. Its associations and symbols include hollow reeds, trees, mountains, grace, connection, inspiration, all colors of the rainbow, and Spirit.

"Listen to your life. See it for the fathomless mystery that it is. In the boredom and pain of it no less than in the excitement and gladness: touch, taste, smell your way to the holy and hidden heart of it because in the last analysis all moments are key moments and life itself is grace."

—FREDERICK BUECHNER

Milagro Strands

I've written about using *milagros* (the name of which comes from the Spanish word for "miracles") before because I love them so—the tiny, base-metal charms that come from Latin American countries, specifically Mexico and Peru. Usually shaped as body parts—eyes, breasts, heads, hearts, hands—but also as animals, vehicles, or even books and pencils for students, *milagros* serve a dual function: They can be symbols of a prayer requested (for healing, for a working car, for good grades), but they can also be symbols of a wish granted, a tangible "thank you" to the Divine for answered prayers.

It is in that capacity that I include them here—as visual thank-you notes, expressions of gratitude for the miracles of one's life. Historically they were placed on altars or shrines and were usually sold outside of churches for use inside as a votive offering, but today you can often find them in museum shops or other stores, or order them over the Internet. They are not only sold alone; you will often find them adorning crosses, boxes, and even articles of jewelry in gold and sterling-silver renditions.

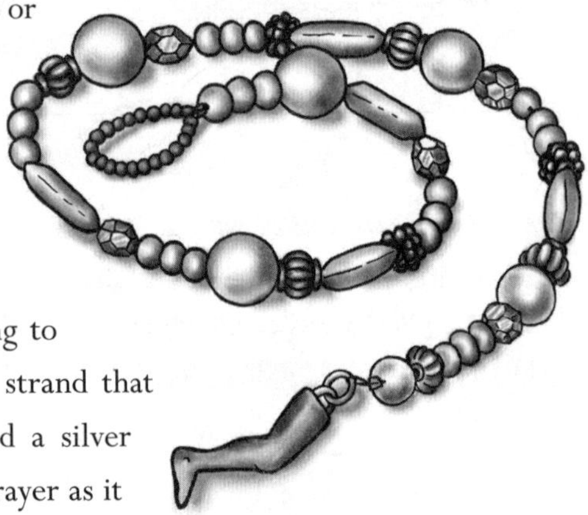

Once when a dear friend of mine was going to have surgery on her leg, I made her a *milagro* strand that included beads in healing shades of green and a silver *milagro* of a leg. For me, it was not so much a prayer as it was an affirmation—giving thanks in advance for an efficacious operation (which it was). It had a little loop of beads on one end into which the *milagro* could be placed; that loop enabled the strand to be hung if desired or worn around the wrist.

If you want to give thanks—even in advance—for the successful conclusion of a health challenge, making a *milagro* strand is a wonderful practice. (To choose colors for their health-giving properties, see the sidebar on page 34.)

Inner Inquiries for Journaling and Reflection

- What in my life needs healing—mental, emotional, spiritual, physical—right now?
- What healing have I had that I have not yet expressed gratitude for? How could I express that gratitude?

DIY: Crafting a Milagro Strand

After you've decided what best symbolizes the area of your life that you want to express gratitude for, choose a compatible *milagro* that will hang at one end of your strand. For instance, a *milagro* of a couple could suggest gratitude for a strong and happy marriage; a *milagro* of a head could suggest gratitude for your education. (For a wide selection of *milagros* to order online and to learn more about their meanings, check out Zanzibar Trading Company at http://zanzibartrading.com/MexicanMilagros.htm) Cut a length of beading wire as long or as short as you want to make your strand and thread the wire through the hole in the top of the *milagro*. Anchor the short end of the wire to the longer side with a crimp bead (a bead used to finish off a piece of jewelry) and secure with crimping pliers. String the beads that you want to include on your strand, leaving enough space on the other end of the wire to make a loop. String a crimp bead at the end, then use smaller beads to create your loop. Push the end of the wire back through the crimp bead and a few of the others at the top of the strand, then use your pliers to squeeze the crimp bead shut and close the loop. You now have a personalized *milagro* strand that you can hang, wear, or simply hold to literally see your answered prayer!

"When we choose not to focus on what is missing from our lives but are grateful for the abundance that's present—love, health, family, friends, work, the joys of nature and personal pursuits that bring us pleasure—the wasteland of illusion falls away and we experience Heaven on earth."

—SARAH BAN BREATHNACH

Origami Cranes

I remember the delight I felt when I found the first tiny star made of iridescent pink paper in my daughter's backpack. What was this sweet little symbol? When I asked her, my daughter—then in elementary school—replied that her teacher's assistant would hand out tiny stars, folded from origami paper, as rewards for good behavior or assignments well done. And not only did she give the stars out, but she also taught her small charges how to make them. It was then that the constellation of stars appeared in our household, galaxies of paper stars, neatly folded (most of the time) in different shades and prints of beautiful Japanese paper, and turning up everywhere.

My daughter had caught the origami bug—and I fed it, buying her origami kits with animal-skin patterned paper so she could make tiny giraffes and zebras. Origami offers a particular enchantment due to its small scale and its simplicity. No glue, tape, or staples necessary; just a few skillful folds, and a menagerie—or a galaxy—is created.

And over the years, gratitude practices have been created from the making of origami cranes. According to Japanese folklore, anyone who folds one thousand origami cranes will have a wish granted to them. This practice was brought to life in a very poignant way in the 1977 children's book *Sadako and the Thousand Paper Cranes* by Eleanor Coerr, which told the true story of Sadako Sasaki, who was two years old when her city of Hiroshima was devastated by the atomic bomb. Within a decade, Sadako was experiencing disturbing symptoms, which were soon diagnosed as leukemia. Familiar with the story of the thousand cranes, and desiring more than anything to be cured of her disease, Sadako began to fold her tiny paper cranes—but she still died ten years after the Hiroshima bombing. Though there are differing accounts as to whether or not Sadako finished her thousand cranes before she passed away, she and her cranes became a symbol of peace—and origami cranes have been the focus for a number of movements related to peace, hope, and healing in all its forms.

One thousand origami cranes remain a good-luck symbol; when they are held together with string they are called *senbazuru*, and are a traditional Japanese wedding gift that symbolizes a wish for one thousand years of happiness and prosperity. *Senbazuru* are often hung in people's homes to bring good fortune.

There are many ways to use origami cranes as a gratitude practice. For a woman named Karen Elaine, who is a breast cancer survivor, making origami cranes and giving them to people who are currently battling serious health challenges is both a gratitude practice and a way to "pay it forward," since she herself received a box of hundreds of origami cranes, each of which represented a prayer for her recovery, while she was grappling with her illness.

Another woman had the idea of making one thousand cranes as a vehicle to count one thousand blessings in her life and documented the process on social media.

No matter how you might choose to work with the practice of the thousand cranes, you will find the process healing in itself, a meditation to the magic that can be created from the mundane. (There are a number of Internet tutorials on how to make an origami crane; one of the clearest is found here: http://www.wikihow.com/Fold-a-Paper-Crane.)

All you need is a heart that wishes—and hands to fold.

Inner Inquiries for Journaling and Reflection

- What are the prayers of my heart right now? What is the wish that I would want granted should the folklore be true?
- What are the thousand blessings of my life? (If you haven't begun to count them, consider doing so while folding origami cranes. With gratitude as your focus, making your own *senbazuru* chain will truly be a symbol of good fortune—all that you have already been blessed with.)

Chapter 3

Gratitude for Wealth and Prosperity

Chapter 3:

Gratitude for Wealth and Prosperity

"We can only be said to be alive in those moments when our hearts are conscious of our treasures."

—THORNTON WILDER

HAVING JUST COVERED HEALTH, LET US MOVE ON TO THE arena of wealth, usually next in line in the longed-for triumvirate of health, wealth, and happiness. When you don't have your health, it usually doesn't matter how much wealth you have—and some would counter that when you don't have wealth, it's hard to feel happy. But does money really buy happiness? Experts in gratitude would say no, that it's not about how much you have but about how much you *appreciate* what you have. As author Dawna Markova wisely wrote, "Gratitude is like a flashlight. If you go out in your yard at night and turn on a flashlight, you suddenly can see what's there. It was always there, but you couldn't see it in the dark."

Therefore, the practices in this section focus on illuminating what's there before us and on broadening our conception of wealth—seeing it not solely as monetary riches, but as anything that makes us feel prosperous and abundant. Sources ranging from the Christian Science Hymnal to Dietrich Bonhoeffer say the same thing—that no matter how much you have, if you are not grateful for it, it will never be enough. Happily for all of us, the reverse is also true—no matter how little we have, if we are grateful for it and truly appreciate it, we will always feel the contentment of having, being, and doing enough.

"I thank you, O God, for your care and protection this day, keeping me from physical harm and spiritual corruption. I now place the work of the day into your hands, trusting that you will redeem my errors and turn my achievements to your glory. And I now ask you to work within me, trusting that you will use the hours of rest to create in me a new heart and a new soul."

—JACOB BOEHME

And mysteriously, our appreciation seems to have a causative effect—gratitude appears to act as a magnet for even more things to be grateful for. Business consultant Tom Peters summarized this phenomenon succinctly: "Celebrate what you want to see more of."

Gratitude Bundles

"Gratitude bundles are a way to put spiritual principles into physical form, making a direct connection between ordinary reality and the Divine," Victoria Marina-Tompkins explains. "I first learned about gratitude bundles from a friend, John Red Crow, a Lakota Indian who taught me the basics of the ritual. I have expanded it over the past twenty-five years with my shamanic groups and find it a very focused and effective manifesting tool."

Victoria had a somewhat circuitous route to her current role as the founder of a shamanic school. She began her career as a freelance violinist, playing for theatrical productions in the San Francisco Bay Area. When her son, Brendan, was born in 1982, she began studying the Orff method of teaching music, and she later started her own music school for children, Tunes for Tots.

It was during her Orff studies that she discovered shamanism through her love of music. Orff classes included body movement, sound, and percussion and felt distinctly tribal to Victoria, as everyone participated together through music, storytelling, and ritual. Soon thereafter she began spiritual studies with Hallie Austen, Karen Vogel (creator with Vicki Noble of the Motherpeace Tarot), Angeles Arrien and Michael Harner.

In 1987 she took the leap and founded her own shamanic school, Flight of the Hawk, in Half Moon Bay, California. She has since expanded her practice to include astrology and intuitive counseling as well as shamanic studies. For Victoria, the practice of gratitude is fundamental to the experience of prosperity: "I think that people in general tend to get a little confused about gratitude. Sometimes, when things aren't working so well in your life, it's hard to feel grateful—there's a tendency to focus on what isn't going well.

"I certainly have had challenges in my life, as many people have, and it was during those times that I would spend more time in nature so I could quiet my mind down enough to realize the innate gift of centering, being comforted by Spirit. I think it was in those moments when I first realized that there is always generosity available—the generosity and goodness of Spirit. And I felt grateful.

"Being grateful for all that is in our lives helps us resist fear and our tendency to look at what isn't working. We see what is positive; gratitude is a way of opening our hearts in each and every moment and fully appreciating what is in our lives, while still remaining open to outcomes that we may not have envisioned but that are rich.

"Abundance and prosperity come in many forms," Victoria reminds us, "including our relationships, work, environments, and creative thought. Many people limit their ideas about prosperity when they think abundance is how much money they have in the bank. I think of abundance as the creative and wonderful experiences we have in our lives—the bounty of quality relationships, enjoying the richness of every day, something as simple as sitting with my Cavalier dogs: That's abundance."

For Victoria, the concept of gratitude includes the element of reciprocity: "Reciprocity is one of the keys to creating abundance in your life. Similar to the yin-yang symbol, reciprocity both gives and receives in equal measure. Becoming aware of giving is very important if you want to receive, as this awareness allows you to step into the natural flow of the Universe. This flow is beautifully illustrated by the figure eight or infinity symbol. Drawing this symbol with your hand in the air shows how energy moves toward you and then away from you, both giving and receiving. Often when a person feels they are not creating what they want in life, it helps to shift focus to giving more, a gesture that is always followed—although not necessarily immediately—by receiving. Once both giving and receiving are a natural way of being, then balance can be restored and abundance will be a natural part of your life."

Having a practice to foster gratitude is so important, Victoria says, because "when we're in the 'what isn't working' space, we're in Fear. And when we move toward the gratitude space, then we're in Love. Fear equals separation, feeling separate; but when we move toward gratitude, then we're experiencing Love—connection.

"And when we experience love and gratitude, then we experience the inner richness that we have—that's abundance! We grow up in this culture thinking that we need other things, that we need to fill ourselves up; but in fact, we all have this inner richness, this inner well inside us—we just get cut off from it. Gratitude practices are a way of bringing us back to that well."

"Have you ever noticed the way it feels to be around grateful people? You feel energized, alive, and inspired to give thanks yourself for the friends, families, and community members that make a difference in your daily living."

—NINA LESOWITZ

Inner Inquiries for Journaling and Reflection

- What do wealth, prosperity, abundance mean to me? Are they the same thing?
- At what times do I feel the most prosperous, the most abundant? What can I do to foster that feeling more often?

DIY: Crafting a Gratitude Bundle for Prosperity and Abundance

Here are Victoria's instructions for making a gratitude bundle:

Gather two or three small objects that represent abundance, prosperity, physical health, connection to the earth, or anything else you would like to express gratitude for. Choose a quiet, sacred space either inside or in nature where you will be undisturbed for thirty minutes. Spread out a small piece of cloth, about 12 x 12 inches, on the floor or table. Ring a bell or chime to begin the ritual.

Ground and center yourself and let go of all distractions and thoughts. You may also want to play calming background music. Once you are ready, pick up one of your objects and whisper over and over what you are grateful for, then place the object on the cloth. Do the same with each object until they are all placed on the cloth.

Visualize the abundance you would like to experience in your life. State it aloud: "I would like to experience ______________. I am grateful for [list the things represented by the objects you have chosen]."

Place a small piece of sage in the bundle. Thank all your ancestors who have walked before you. Wrap up the cloth and tie it with a piece of ribbon or twine. Sit with your gratitude bundle in your lap or hands while continuing to visualize abundance and prosperity in your life. Feel gratitude for all that you have in your life now!

Ring the bell again to close the ritual. Then find a place for the gratitude bundle in your environment so you can see it every day and remember your gratitude. Ring the bell or chime as you walk by and say out loud what you are feeling grateful for.

Victoria says, "This practice honors what is and acknowledges the sacred river that runs within all of us and connects us to Spirit. It is life affirming; it says *yes* and opens us to the infinite abundance that is always present."

"I'm not the holiest person you've ever met, but I thank God for what I've had and what I've got. I'm grateful for it all—the windows, the light, the street, and the cars. I know I've been looked after in this life."

—B. B. KING

Crafting a Gratitude Practice

"If you're just starting a process, I suggest writing down three things you're grateful for when you first wake up. This helps you to develop a focus on gratitude. I also will have clients get a little jar or box and write down the things they're grateful for and put them in there—it's a way of connecting their lives with these spiritual concepts.

"I would suggest that you start thinking about gratitude more, so it's part of your daily life, not just on weekends. Read a book where there's a prayer or thought for each day, because gratitude is a more reflective state. I also would encourage people to speak it out loud. So if you're having an experience that you're grateful for, say it so that it becomes part of your way of life. All of these suggestions shift your focus away from the negative and toward what *is* working."

—VICTORIA MARINA-TOMPKINS

PROSPERITY ALTARS

Living in San Francisco as I do, where people of Asian descent number more than one-third of the population, it is relatively common when walking into a hair and nail salon or restaurant to see a tiny altar on a shelf or even on the floor. Measuring a little over one foot tall and one foot wide, these small temples are usually red and gold in color, featuring a deity inside and attendant offerings: fruit, flowers, incense, coins. They are there to bring good fortune to the business, to give gratitude to the Ultimate Boss.

Though I have never created an altar specifically for the intention of prosperity, I have made and continue to make small altars around me to focus on particular points of reflection—and if you stop to think about it, really every altar is in some way referencing the abundance that is around us always. For instance, every time I have written a book, I have created a tiny altar under my computer keyboard; though some elements remain constant—a colorful lenticular card that depicts Lakshmi (Hindu goddess of love and prosperity) on one side and Saraswati (goddess of wisdom and arts) on the other; an iridescent fossilized ammonite spiral; four tiny porcelain owls in white, yellow, gold, and orange that my daughter bought me in Chinatown; a tin of earth from a healing site in Chimayo, New Mexico; a carved stone with "All things are possible" etched on it—some other elements change. During the time I have worked on the book you are reading now, other items have been added; for instance, because this is a book on gratitude, I included a tiny card, 2 inches square, on which the words "Thank you" are printed. (I also have a prominent flash drive in the shape of Wonder Woman that saves my drafts!) And just typing those descriptions of my altar items makes me happy. My altar reminds me of all the riches of my life: the studies and work that nourish me, the travel experiences that deepen me, the relationships that moor me.

If you are considering creating a prosperity altar, you might want to start by thinking about which area of your life you wish to highlight. Is this an altar to give thanks for all the prosperity currently in your life? Or is it an altar to invite prosperity into your life, giving gratitude in advance for answered prayers? Will this altar be in your home, or in your workplace? If, like Asian entrepreneurs, you hope to manifest more prosperity in your own business, what better way to stay focused on your goals and dreams than to create an altar for it—preferably small enough to be unobtrusive and perhaps even private, but with symbols that remind you of the larger picture, the *what* of your business and the *why*.

Crafting a prosperity altar of gratitude for a business, or an important project, or life in general, is a way to remind us of what's most good, true, and beautiful in our lives—a way of affirming abundance, even when we feel lack. It's a way of remembering that we always partner with the Divine, whether we're sole proprietors or not.

Inner Inquiries for Journaling and Reflection

- Do I have a tabletop or a corner of my desk or dresser that displays objects that remind me of prosperity and abundance, of the fullness of my life?
- Where could I place an altar—and what symbols would I use—to invite prosperity into my work or important projects?

Common Symbols of Prosperity

There are many symbols of prosperity found in various cultures, particularly Asian cultures, including the following:

BLOODSTONE: If you want to place something under your computer, or to have as part of a traveling altar that is carried with you, then bloodstone might be just the thing. Its green color with shiny flecks represents the green of dollar bills and the sparkle of coins; it also represents new growth, the flourishing shoots of spring.

JADE PLANT: In China, jade is highly valued and a symbol of wealth and status—and thus the jade plant, whose leaves look like jade, is seen as a good-luck symbol. Jade plants are often placed near the entrances of businesses to attract prosperity.

MANEKI NEKO: This "Beckoning Cat" with its upraised paw, which originated in Japan in the 19th century but also is used in Chinese businesses, is a well-known symbol of good luck. It is believed that a cat with an upraised right paw attracts money, and one with an upraised left paw attracts customers, but sometimes that association is reversed. Maybe it's best to buy two maneki neko, just to hedge your bets!

MONEY TOAD: In many Asian cultures, the frog or toad is said to bring healing and prosperity. The money toad or fortune frog, called "Chan Chu" in Chinese, is considered particularly powerful for ushering in abundance. Often depicted with a coin in its mouth, the money toad is acknowledged as the pet of the Chinese god of wealth, and should be placed near a cash register for prosperous transactions.

SALMON: In the Pacific Northwest, some Native American tribes consider salmon to be a symbol of prosperity and renewal. Some people eat salmon on the first day of the year for financial good luck in the days ahead.

Abundance Boards

We all have some kind of bulletin board somewhere, maybe in the cubicle where we work, or in the kitchen where we eat—a thumbtack-studded depository of calendars, memos, helpful phone numbers, appointment reminder cards, vacation-spot postcards from friends, and other ephemera from our filled-to-the-max lives.

But what if we used a bulletin board for a different kind of reminder—as a tool for remembering all that we have to be grateful for? That's the idea behind an abundance board—to create something that hangs before you, replete with images of all the blessings of your life. Both a cause for celebration and an intention for manifestation, abundance boards work on the principle outlined by doctor and author Christiane Northrup: "Feeling grateful or appreciative of someone or something in your life actually attracts more of the things that you appreciate and value into your life." And as author Ellen Vaughn writes, "The more we thank, the more we see to be thankful for. Gratitude is the lens that reveals God's incredible grace at work. It is the key to tangible, everyday joy."

Inner Inquiries for Journaling and Reflection

- The word *abundance* comes from a Latin root meaning "to overflow." In what arenas of my life does my cup truly "runneth over"?
- Do I really *see* all that I have to be grateful for on a daily basis?

DIY: Crafting an Abundance Board

When creating an abundance board, you can use a traditional cork bulletin board, but consider decorating it in a way that honors what you're acknowledging. Use a beautiful paint color to cover the cork and the frame, or buy a fancier, gilded frame to place around the corkboard. You can find special thumbtacks to use when displaying your items, or make your own by gluing buttons, shapes, or charms to the flat head of a thumbtack.

Things to display might include photographs of cherished family members and friends, tickets to an upcoming concert date, a certificate awarded at school or in the workplace, or a greeting card from an admirer. Whatever you're thankful for, whatever makes you remember the richness of your life in all its fullness, that's what you should include—and you should study it, if not add to it, daily. And if the things you have to be grateful for are too many to include on a single board, then consider hanging an abundance board in every room of your house!

Prosperity Candles

A candle has been a spiritual tool for millennia because it literally is what it seeks to invoke: light. No matter how many electric lights might be found in our dwellings, candles will always have a place at the table, both literally and figuratively. There is something entrancing about staring at a candle flame, something comforting about the ritual of lighting a match and touching it to a wick.

Candles can be used for many purposes. For some, they may simply be a fragrant addition to the home décor; for others, they might mark a period of meditation. In some folk and faith traditions, candles are burned with the hope of drawing a desire forward, such as the desire for prosperity; here, we are going to look at using a candle as a means to give thanks.

Sages around the world have commented that in order to experience more prosperity, one needs to be grateful for what one already has. Rather than craft a candle to bring more abundance to you, how about creating a candle that will remind you of all that you have? You might consider lighting it in the morning, during your devotional time, or in the evening, before you go to bed. You might want to combine it with a thankfulness prayer, such as this one by Ralph Waldo Emerson (adapt if necessary to reflect your conception of the Divine):

For each new morning with its light,
For rest and shelter of the night,
For health and food,
For love and friends,
For everything Thy goodness sends,
Father in heaven,
We thank thee.

Or simply light the candle every time you need to be reminded of the prosperity in your life—by making your own candle, you will draw upon the memories of the gratitude you felt when you made it. Breathe in its fragrance, and let the light in.

"Gratitude is the state of mind of thankfulness. As it is cultivated, we experience an increase in our 'sympathetic joy,' our happiness at another's happiness. Just as in the cultivation of compassion, we may feel the pain of others, so we may begin to feel their joy as well. And it doesn't stop there."

—STEPHEN LEVINE

Inner Inquiries for Journaling and Reflection

- What places, people, and things in my life make me feel truly prosperous?
- What are the colors and objects that symbolize prosperity to me?

DIY: Crafting a Prosperity Candle

Candle-making is more simple than it might seem; you can use recycled wax and melt it into a clear glass container, placing a wick (or, depending on the size of the container, two or three wicks) into the center. To truly make it a prosperity candle, add some green, gold, or silver color to your wax with liquid or solid dyes (you can even use your kids' old crayons!); add coins or charms that represent things for which you are grateful, such as a car or a house; use an essential oil that is associated with prosperity and abundance, such as cinnamon, ginger, or orange; and add sparkling glitter to the candle's top layer before it cools completely.

Cornucopias of Plenty

Technically speaking, it is redundant to say "cornucopias of plenty," as the word *cornucopia* comes from a Latin phrase meaning "horn of plenty." Cornucopias suggest an element of inexhaustible riches; according to Greek mythology, the cornucopia was a magical goat's horn that would always refill with whatever food or drink its owner desired. But when it comes to expressing gratitude, it doesn't hurt to underscore the idea of plenty, and what better way to do that than to make our own Cornucopias of Plenty?

A staple decoration on Thanksgiving tables, cornucopias are hollow, horn-shaped cones into which fruit, nuts, and other treats can be stuffed. Or, if purely decorative, they serve as representations of our inner or outer harvest—all that we have cultivated and gathered in the preceding months.

If you're looking for a definitive symbol of prosperity and abundance, there's nothing more concise than a cornucopia. And because of their simple shape, cornucopias can be made out of just about any material imaginable—ranging from paper (a craft you could do with your children or grandchildren) to raffia, bread dough to reeds.

To craft your Cornucopia of Plenty, first decide how you want to use it and what specifically you want it to represent. If it's something that you want to keep out year-round, then you'll probably want something in a bigger scale, made of materials that will last. There are many tutorials available on the Internet for making your own cornucopia out of the materials listed above; you could also buy a cornucopia in a craft store and embellish it with paint, ribbon, and charms of your choosing.

Since you are making and using your cornucopia as a gratitude practice, you can fill it with representations of all the wonderful things that fill your life—photographs of family members, small figurines of a dog or cat, symbols of your passions (flower seeds, paint-brushes, a tennis ball), a favorite poem or prayer. You can keep adding to your cornucopia throughout the year, and watch as it overflows with the abundance that is your life!

Inner Inquiries for Journaling and Reflection

- What have I cultivated—and harvested—so far this year?
- In what area or areas of my life do I feel a sense of inexhaustible plenty? In what area or areas of my life would I *like* to feel a sense of inexhaustible plenty?

Chapter 4

GRATITUDE FOR HOME

Chapter 4:

Gratitude for Home

"Nowadays, people are so jeezled up. If they took some chamomile tea and spent more time rocking on the porch in the evening listening to the liquid song of the hermit thrush, they might enjoy life more."

—TASHA TUDOR

FAMED CHILDREN'S-BOOK ILLUSTRATOR TASHA TUDOR WAS right—people are so "jeezled up" these days. And because of that, the concept of home—of a place we can enter, be ourselves in, rest and renew and reflect in, seems more important than ever. Who can claim to have watched *The Wizard of Oz* (even for the umpteenth time) and *not* been moved by Dorothy's quest to go home? Perhaps some of the longevity of that cinematic and cultural icon is due to the fact that we all have felt like strangers in a strange land at some point in our lives—and there's nothing like being away from it for us to realize that there truly is no place like home.

One anonymous Internet poet knows the value of home—in fact, this poet is so appreciative of the comforts of home that she or he has written a number of prayers in gratitude for it. In one, called "Thank You for Shelter," the poet gives thanks not only for always having a shelter in which to sleep, but for being born in a hospital, and for being able to attend school ("the ones that gave me a safe place to learn and study, and free food when I was hungry, with a backyard which I was able to play in with my other classmates during recess"). When was the last time you gave real gratitude for the gift of shelter? Or for being born in a hospital, or having a safe school to attend? And, if you didn't have those particular experiences, what forms of shelter *could* you be grateful for?

Recently a wonderful essay called "Give Me Gratitude or Give Me Debt," published by Glennon Doyle Melton on her blog (www.momastery.com), was circulated on social media. This essay skillfully showed how we can start to doubt our abundance when what we have is filtered through other people's negative gazes—and how it can seem to magically increase when we look at what we have through eyes of gratitude. Glennon's subject was her kitchen, which appeared rather shabby and charmless until she took stock of what it contained—from the convenience of a microwave to a floor on which her family could dance. As Glennon wrote in her essay: "I remembered this passage from Thoreau's *Walden*: 'I say beware of all enterprises that require new clothes and not a new wearer of the clothes.' *Walden* reminds me that when I feel lacking—I don't need new things, I need new eyes with which to see the things I already have."

Wise words for living a life of gratitude. In this section, you'll read more about what the comforts of home can mean to people—and how they keep looking at what they have with new eyes.

Gratitude Bowls

Suzanne Stovall Vinson is a minister—but her choice of occupational venue may surprise you. Ordained in the Baptist tradition, Suzanne spent a number of years in church ministry but left when she found herself being called back to another place that had always been a church of sorts for her: the table in her home. Now she leads art and spirituality retreats, as well as bereavement support. "My ministry has always been around the table," Suzanne says.

And why? "Home is where everything begins," Suzanne explains, "and sometimes there are memories of home that need to be healed or resurrected in some way. I come from Mississippi, the Hospitality State, and that was an essential part of life—all the rhythms of life came from home. My grandparents lived next door, so their house was also mine; for me, home means the people."

Suzanne has cherished memories of home from the time before her mother's remarriage; after that, things changed dramatically. She remembers, "The idea of safety had always revolved around home—and then there were a stepfather and stepsisters who I didn't get along with; I was interrupted by other entities in my own home and had to learn how to deal with those truths. During those years, at times my church was where I would be 'at home'; I would spend Wednesday nights there for dinner. And I was invited to live in different homes during college.

"This gave me such gratitude for the responses of others who really cared for me in the way I needed to be cared for. And so, I brought my people near me. They helped shape me and kept me from going down different routes. I've always looked at myself as a gatherer, and a preparer, of food and hospitality.

"When I attended seminary in Richmond, Virginia, Richmond became my own place; I could make it exactly what I needed it to be. I created a community with my husband, with my church, around tables, and then *I* started gathering folks who needed to be seen and heard around *my* table. I feel at home around the table."

Suzanne's practice with a gratitude bowl was sparked by a passage in Rachel Naomi Remen's book *Kitchen Table Wisdom*; after she read it, Suzanne became inspired to take a bowl and fill it up with running water every morning. Suzanne counsels, "As you are filling it, reflect on what fills you up, what drains you, what gives you life, what takes your life away."

Suzanne uses her gratitude bowl to acknowledge all of these things as the bowl fills; then she puts the filled bowl out during the day "to hold all that the day holds." At the end of the day, she empties the water in the bowl out onto the earth, as a signal to herself to rest. She then places it upside down until it is time to refill it the following morning.

It's an interesting practice, Suzanne says: "What fills us up sometimes drains us, too, and gratitude is a practice of being grateful for what you have. Not everything that looks like pain is pain; sometimes it's pain with blessings."

Suzanne uses an old enamel bowl of her grandmother's to which her grandfather affixed a nut and bolt to to keep it together. She calls it her meditation bowl. She also had a ceramic bowl made by an artist that, she says, "essentially has my whole life carved into it"—it is adorned with concentric circles, spirals, a sparrow, and patterned lace to represent old and new, with the word "be" imprinted on the bottom and the word "create" carved on the outside. Suzanne also had a family bowl made, which has representations of her ancestry; and she has made a blessing bowl for her daughter.

Whether you use a bowl that you make or one that was crafted by another, gratitude bowls can be fashioned from any material. In a bereavement group that Suzanne led, a member decided to crochet a gratitude bowl—and delighted in the metaphor, applicable to life, when she discovered that turning the bowl inside out actually strengthened it.

You can also use other vessels for your gratitude practice, Suzanne notes—you could fill a mason jar or water bottle with your meditation water, so that you actually consume it during the day.

Whether we drink it or simply notice it, perhaps peering into a gratitude bowl every now and then to see our own reflections, or making a habit of filling up a vessel and then emptying it, can bring us back in touch on a daily basis with the ways in which our cups truly runneth over.

Inner Inquiries for Journaling and Reflection

- Where is the place where I feel most "at home"? What is it about that place that nourishes me so?
- What simple practice could I incorporate into my day, into my home, that will help me to track the blessings of the day?

DIY: Crafting a Gratitude Bowl

If you want to explore this practice, you might want to start by looking around your house and seeing if there is already a bowl that holds meaning for you—such as Suzanne's grandmother's enamel bowl. You might also decide whether you want your container to hold water (and if so, whether you want to consume the water throughout the day or simply let it stand) or if you want to work with a container that serves as a metaphor, such as the crocheted Gratitude Bowl the woman in Suzanne's group made.

If you decide to make your own bowl, note whether your materials are watertight. But know that even if they can't hold water, they can hold much meaning. You could make bowls with natural elements, allowing imagery to come to your mind to dictate how to shape it most meaningfully. Or you could use a craft clay like Crayola Model Magic or compounds that air-dry, allowing you to press objects or carve words into your bowl before it hardens. You could also buy a bowl and embellish it with paints or plastic "gems" or other decorations—whatever helps you to remember gratitude for all that fills up your day.

> "The generosity of God in sharing the goodness of creation with us can elicit only one possible response—that of gratitude."
>
> —ESTHER DE WAAL

Crafting a Gratitude Practice

"I have two thoughts. The first is that with any addition in life, sometimes you need to subtract something too—so if you're adding a gratitude practice, then maybe there's something that needs to go away. And then, just start with one; just add being grateful for one thing, or naming it at the end of the day—whatever it is, even if it's the same thing. As you have that practice of gratitude, it starts changing you, because you have that habit of looking for it.

"Another practice I have comes from my Eternal Home: I listen for wisdom daily—the collective wisdom, Spirit wisdom. At the end of the day, I make a piece of art with the words I've heard. I think we do this to give ourselves life."

—SUZANNE STOVALL VINSON

SABBATH CANDLEHOLDERS

"Throughout all generations
we will render thanks unto Thee
And declare Thy praise,
Evening, morning and noon
For our lives which are in Thy care,
For our souls which are in Thy keeping
For Thy miracles which we witness daily,
And for Thy wondrous deeds and blessings
Toward us at all times."

—JEWISH SABBATH PRAYER

Aimee Golant is an acclaimed artist and metalsmith whose Jewish heritage has always informed her art. She began her career somewhat unexpectedly when she learned of her grandparents' experience during the Holocaust and found herself making *mezuzahs*, small cases meant to be attached to doorposts, in which scrolls containing passages from the Torah have been placed. Aimee's artwork now encompasses interfaith art installations, jewelry, and other items—including the beautiful silver lotus candleholders that she made to use for a particular purpose: to denote the beginning of Shabbat/ Sabbath ("Shabbat" is the Hebrew word for "Sabbath"), and to give thanks for light and a welcome day of rest.

Aimee's candleholders in the shape of lotuses are an interesting choice to celebrate the Sabbath; she notes that the lotus image is never found in Judaica, while it is often found in Eastern religions, but for her there is a connection. "The lotus rises pure and white out of the mud—it is a symbol of being reborn each time, made clean. I see the Sabbath as helping us to do that—but for me, it's also a personal symbol. I see my work as being like the lotus, since it came from the mud of my grandparents' experience in the Holocaust."

For Aimee, the practice of Shabbat/Sabbath is vitally important, and every week during its celebration she sings a Hebrew song that translates as "Good things will come to those who take the Sabbath." Aimee believes that, yes, good things come: enlightenment and prosperity—the prosperity that results from connecting inwardly with gratitude. When doing this, you realize your inner prosperity.

The lighting of the Shabbat candle is important, Aimee says, because by doing this you are carving out the space—you are preparing for this time of rest. Aimee explains, "It's one of the Ten Commandments, but we don't think of it that way, we think of it as optional—but we don't think of not killing someone as optional! It's a commandment because taking a Sabbath is so important."

Working with a special candle and candleholder to mark this time lends itself to a number of meditative practices, Aimee points out. "We are giving gratitude for light when we look at the candlelight. And then there's the larger association of God as light. Many people use candles as a focus for meditating, looking at the flame—and it really doesn't matter if you're meditating for twenty-five minutes twice a day or for the Shabbat period of twenty-five hours; what's important is that you're carving out the time to focus inward and focus on gratitude. In the Jewish tradition, it's about making sure that you're spending ample time with family and with home."

Inner Inquiries for Journaling and Reflection

* Do I have a regular period of Sabbath time right now? If not, why not? How could I create that for myself each week?
* How can I create moments of rest in my days? What small ritual would support me in remembering to stop even for five minutes in the course of my day—an alarm on my cell phone? A note on my computer screen: "Be still and know that I am God"?

DIY: Crafting Sabbath Candleholders

If, unlike Aimee, you are not blessed with the talent of metalworking, there are still ways to create your own candleholders to celebrate the Sabbath. Aimee suggests creating *luminarias*, intricately cut paper bags that hold sand and tea lights within, or making your own candleholders out of clay that can be fired (if you have access to a kiln) or air-dried.

You can also make a special candleholder from an existing one found in a craft store, even a glass votive holder, by embellishing it with painted words, symbols, or charms. Aimee counsels thinking about how long the candle will be able to burn (in the Shabbat tradition, candles burn for three hours and are not supposed to be blown out). Consider decorating your candleholder with symbols for the feminine face of God, as the Sabbath is seen as allowing Shekhinah, the feminine presence of God, into our lives.

Celebratory Platters

When I think back to my wedding and the eclectic nature of the gifts we received (which was not surprising, given that we had registries at both Neiman Marcus and Pier 1 Imports!), it turns out that one of my favorite gifts is still in use today, atop our refrigerator and holding fresh fruit: a ceramic platter painted for the occasion by my then-new nieces and nephew. On this platter are their names and the symbols that were meaningful to them back in elementary school: an orange dragonfly, a yellow moon and green peace sign, a blue fish.

The proliferation of paint-it-yourself ceramic studios underscores the appeal of personalizing a plate or platter; it's a lovely thing to have a special plate or platter that you made yourself or received from a loved one. But there's a way to take this even deeper, by creating a platter that details all that you're grateful for—something on which your blessings are metaphorically heaped! And these require no visit to a ceramic studio to begin the process or return visit to pick up the finished item after it's been fired; these platters are made in your own home.

The kinds of platters we're exploring here are celebratory platters—ready-made porcelain platters (you can find them in a dollar store) on which your blessings are written in indelible, permanent ink. You could make several celebratory platters—each member of the family could create their own—or you could simply adorn a single platter with quotations of gratefulness for blessings large and small. ("One must ask children and birds how cherries and strawberries taste," from Johann Wolfgang von Goethe, is a particularly charming sentiment for a celebratory platter!)

Perhaps there's no better way than with a plate or personalized platter, brought out at special gatherings and celebrations, to truly prove the words by W. J. Cameron: "A thankful heart hath a continual feast."

Inner Inquiries for Journaling and Reflection

- Do I have a ritual for taking a review of all the good that's occurred in the previous year—in my life in general (birthday reflection), in my marriage (anniversary reflection), or in other areas?
- What are the things that I want to remember always? What are the blessings that are "written on my heart"?

DIY: Crafting Celebratory Platters

First, decide what you want to create. A platter is nice because it gives you more space to write on, but you could also choose a plate, a bowl, or even a mug. As noted above, there's no need to find the fancy stuff—just look for the plain white offerings in the dollar or discount store. Then pick up a pack of Sharpie permanent pens—and it is important that they are the Sharpie brand pens, not other permanent pens, as the ink of some of those has been known to flake off later. You can also use porcelain-paint markers. Next, express your thankfulness. If you are making a platter to celebrate birthdays, write down all the blessings that life has offered you. If you're making it to celebrate anniversaries, write down what you love about each other, and include your spouse's name in the descriptions (e.g., "I love David's laugh"; "I love Mary's singing in the shower"). If you like, you can also create designs. Once you have finished embellishing your plate, it's time to make those words last for all eternity—or the closest approximation we have—by baking it in the oven. Please note: Do *not* preheat the oven and then put your item in, as this can cause your item to break. You must always put your decorated item in a cold oven, *then* set it to 350 degrees and bake it for thirty minutes. Set an oven alarm to be sure of the baking time. When the alarm rings, turn off the oven, but leave your item in it to cool down; this will keep your item from breaking from the sudden temperature change.

"Plato said more than 2,500 years ago, 'A grateful mind is a great mind which eventually attracts to itself great things.' A tremendous insight! The grateful person is great because he or she has turned on all the lights within."

—ERIC BUTTERWORTH

Gratitude Goodies

Though I am not a cook myself (unless you count a mean pasta and fabulous scrambled eggs!), I do make a point of whipping up family recipes from scratch on at least a couple of occasions per year: the two kinds of Christmas cookies that my mother used to make, one of them a recipe from her own mother; and, to celebrate my father's maternal lineage, Swedish pancakes on New Year's Day—and on any other special occasion for which they are requested.

We think of crafting foodstuffs around the holidays, for a celebration—but what about making the treats a vehicle for celebrating all the blessings in our lives? This idea first occurred to me when I saw a pin on Pinterest about making gratitude fortune cookies—finding a fortune-cookie recipe and then tucking affirmations of gratitude (you could also list particular things for which you're grateful) inside. And then I thought of the Victorian tradition of baking charms inside a wedding cake—still celebrated today with the Southern tradition of the wedding pull, in which the cake charms are attached to satin ribbons.

> "I am grateful for what I am and have. My thanksgiving is perpetual . . . . O how I laugh when I think of my vague indefinite riches. No run on my bank can drain it, for my wealth is not possession but enjoyment."
>
> —HENRY DAVID THOREAU

Why not craft a new tradition for yourself or your family by making baked goods not only sweet, but symbolic of all the sweetness in your life? For those in a hurry, you could simply buy a tube of ready-made cake frosting and write your gratitude affirmations or blessings on a dozen cupcakes. There are many delicious ways of celebrating gratitude through the craft of baking—see what gratitude goodies you can cook up yourself!

Inner Inquiries for Journaling and Reflection:

- Where do I find the sweetness in life? What is sweet to me?
- What symbol best represents that sweetness to me?

Meanings of Wedding-Cake Charms

If you like the idea of baking a cake with charms that represent things you're grateful for in your life—or things you're hoping will soon be a part of your life—here is a list of some common charm meanings:

AIRPLANE: You will travel and have many adventures.

ANCHOR: You will experience love that is steady and true.

ANGEL: You have a protector that watches over you.

BABY BOTTLE: You will be blessed with many children.

BIRD: A new opportunity is coming to you.

CASTLE: You will live happily ever after!

COIN: You will enjoy riches.

CROWN: You will find your Prince (or Princess) Charming.

FLEUR-DE-LIS: Your life will be prosperous.

FLOWER: Something new (often love) is blossoming in your life.

HEART: You will experience true love.

KITE: Something fun is coming to you!

MUSICAL INSTRUMENT: Your life will be harmonious.

SEASHELL: You will have a life of timeless beauty.

STAR: Your dreams will come true.

SUN: Your future is bright.

TELEPHONE: Good news will soon come calling!

"Praised be my Lord for our Mother the Earth,
which sustains us and keeps us and brings forth diverse fruits,
And flowers of many colors—and grass."

—SAINT FRANCIS OF ASSISI

Spirit Houses

Hailing from Burma, Cambodia, Laos, and Thailand, these miniature houses are small and intricate, usually carved out of teak with exuberant scrollwork, around which offerings to the gods are placed—fruit, flowers. They are spirit houses, dollhouse-sized dwellings or temples that are meant to be displayed outside one's house so that helpful spirits have a place to reside. One stands outside my house right now. I bought it at a folk-art store in Berkeley when my husband and I bought our house across the bay in San Francisco. It had been such a journey of faith, to unexpectedly enter the crazy housing market in my beautiful, popular city, that I wanted something outside our front door to demonstrate the gratitude we felt for finally—after looking at no less than seventy-five properties and bidding on two others that we lost—ending up with a home that was nicer than we ever dreamed possible.

I cheated a little with the offerings—the flower outside my spirit house is a yellow silk hibiscus blossom that is meant to be pinned to a lapel, and the orange is a plastic one that our insurance company handed out at a street fair to promote good nutrition—but the gratitude is no less heartfelt. Almost every day, when I drive up with my daughter after school, we both say, "Here we are at the pretty house!"

That's the purpose of a spirit house—to remind the people displaying it to give thanks to the Divine of their understanding for their blessings of house and home. For some in Southeast Asia, the offerings are meant to appease the gods, so that no harm will fall to your house, but when researching this book, I was happy to discover that spirit houses can also be symbols of gratitude. In an article that appeared in the *Phnom Penh Post*, a man was quoted as saying that they work for "people [who] wish to show gratitude to the angels who give life to people through the earth, wind, fire, and water." In addition, this source said, the spirit houses have a connection to our lineage, serving as a focus to "pray to the angels to bless the spirits of [our] ancestors."

Spirit houses can be as simple or elaborate as desired; they can be gilded like a temple or left as simple teakwood. When they are not made of teak, they are often painted with a color that denotes the day of the week on which the owner of the house was born; according to this system, Monday is represented by the color yellow, Tuesday by pink, Wednesday by green, Thursday by gold, Friday by blue, Saturday by purple, and Sunday by red.

I have been so taken by the idea of spirit houses that I used them as the focus of an afternoon workshop that I once conducted. I had found house-shaped frames about one foot tall, divided into "rooms," on sale at a Japanese dry-goods shop, and I invited my participants to furnish their small spirit houses with images and representations of the things they love or want to focus on the most. For instance, in my spirit house, the attic space—the triangular top of the house—was adorned with a bead printed with the word "God."

If you are interested in this practice of working with spirit houses, you could try buying or building a small three-dimensional one and outfitting it in the way that calls to you. In Southeast Asian countries, often small figures are included. Or you could work two-dimensionally, by crafting a house shape, dividing it up into rooms (think of a wooden sock-drawer divider), and adorning it with symbols of your gratitude for what each room brings—a red heart to symbolize your significant other in the bedroom section, perhaps, or dollhouse-food items in the kitchen section, to represent gratitude for never being hungry. Working with a spirit house reminds us, in the pointed words of a wise Internet pundit, that some people are praying for the very things we take for granted.

Inner Inquiries for Journaling and Reflection

- What does my home mean to me? Have I ever had a gratitude practice that focuses specifically on my home?
- What small thing could I incorporate into my life to remind me of the blessing of home?

Chapter 5

GRATITUDE FOR VOCATIONS AND AVOCATIONS

Chapter 5:

Gratitude for Vocations and Avocations

"No matter what accomplishments you achieve, somebody helped you."

—ALTHEA GIBSON

THE WORD *VOCATION* COMES FROM A LATIN ROOT MEANING "to call; a calling." Generally speaking, a vocation is something that we've been called to, a type of work, such as a religious vocation or call to teach. Avocations, on the other hand, are considered something we do for pleasure, something that is not our work but our hobby, which we do in our leisure time.

Yet in a world in which the Buddhist concept of "right livelihood"—work in which love, devotion, and service are employed—is often referred to, and in which Joseph Campbell's exhortation to "follow your bliss" is often applied to finding one's right livelihood, the two concepts have become somewhat intertwined. Many people are not content these days to compartmentalize their lives so clearly; they want their job to be their bliss and to know firsthand that—as Confucius allegedly noted—"if you love what you do, you'll never work another day in your life."

So no matter which camp you fall into—whether your job is just a job and you follow your passions in your leisure time, or your work is something you'd do whether you got paid or not—there are practices in this section that will help you to better appreciate and give gratitude for your calling, that which you have been called to do. And don't stop at giving gratitude for your vocation and avocation—remember to give thanks for everything that is done all around you by people seen and unseen; give thanks for those whose work contributes dramatically to the quality of yours. That in itself is a powerful gratitude practice; as no less a sage than Albert Einstein once said, "A hundred times every day I remind myself that my inner and outer life depend on the labors of other men, living and dead, and that I must exert myself in order to give in the same measure as I have received and am still receiving."

Honey Jars

As writer and transformation teacher Jamie Walters notes on her blog, it should make us feel better that the tenth-century monk, mystic, and Cistercian Abbot Bernard of Clairvaux—who would seem to have already figured out this question of vocation—would wake up each morning and, as he rose from his pallet, would ask, "Bernard, Bernard, why have you come here?"

As someone who mentors and guides people through the process of change, Jamie has heard this question come up many, many times before—and she herself has grappled with it, having been the founder and owner of a successful big-city consulting company and now working primarily alone as a writer and guide through the transformative process, and having undergone many transformations herself along the way. Jamie says, "For me, vocation and avocation are like two sides of the same coin. And what I've seen is that so much of what is happening even with clients is about vocation—when what we've built has fallen apart."

During those times, Jamie feels, a gratitude practice is key; either giving thanks for what is, or in anticipation of what can—and it is affirmed, *will*—be. Jamie has found the making of a honey jar to be a helpful practice and reflection:

"A honey jar can be used for a lot of things—there are all kinds of variations of this. I learned this practice from a friend who comes from the hoodoo tradition of the southeastern United States, a confluence of Cajun, African, Christian, and European influences." The purpose of a honey jar is to invite synchronicities, ask for clarity, and give gratitude. "As a gratitude practice," Jamie explains, "the gratitude is in the practice of it, the practice is the prayer. It's a way of giving thanks either in retrospect or in anticipation.

"Say you want to make a honey jar for your vocation—for instance, writing. You want to get a small jar of raw honey, which is a natural preservative, meaning anything you put into it will not go rancid." Jamie suggests reading the ingredients label to be sure it contains only raw honey, without corn syrup or other additives, which do not have the same preservative qualities. "Empty the honey out into another container; maybe leave a third of it in the jar. And then pick little things that are symbolic of your gratitude for your vocation—just like our ancestors might have kept in a bog. For example, you might want to put in a small piece of rose quartz to symbolize staying in your heart when you write; a charm that's in the shape of a quill pen or book; perhaps something natural, like a leaf or rosebud. You want to have five or six—but probably not more than ten—objects in your honey jar. In one of my honey jars, I have a couple of stones, a charm, a sprig of a plant, and a little butterfly I found that had died, as a symbol of transformation—things like that.

"And then on a little piece of paper, which could be pretty paper or parchment, write a prayer of thanks; you could also include poetry. The piece of paper should be no more than 3 inches square. Roll it up like a scroll, fasten it with a piece of twine, and put it in your honey jar. Then refill the honey jar with honey up to the rim. In the old days, honey was considered an offering to the Divine. Plus, if you buy it locally, you're supporting the economy.

"Then burn a tiny birthday candle or tea light and seal it to the Honey Jar with wax, saying a prayer or mantra if you like as you seal it. Fire symbolizes the transporting or changing of energy from the material; the transformation of the prayer from my heart to God's ears. While the candle is burning, you want to be in the presence of the honey jar and pray or journal or take a ceremonial bath until it burns out by itself. Ideally you wouldn't blow it out." Jamie suggests covering the lid with aluminum foil if it's plastic rather than metal.

Having made the honey jar, some people put it on their personal altar; some bury it deep in the earth (deep enough that animals won't be able to reach it if it breaks). "In doing this," Jamie says, "we're planting the seed for the continuation, the evolution, of whatever it is we're honey-jarring. We're doing it in divine gratitude or anticipation of our great work in the world."

That's the foundational practice, Jamie notes—but you can also make it your own by augmenting the practice, which might include decorating the honey jar or putting a tiny plant on top of the lid so that it becomes a living prayer. The honey jar, Jamie says, is basically a prayer for the sweetening of situations, or for healing, since honey itself is healing.

Should you keep a honey jar indefinitely? Jamie feels that you should check your intuitive knowing about that. If your honey jar represents an ongoing prayer, you might want to keep it—

but dust it, and occasionally burn a fresh candle on top of it, to keep it "alive." When your prayer has been answered, or if a new direction has been shown to you, Jamie recommends burying the contents, then washing and recycling the jar. For those who make a practice of expressing gratitude through making a honey jar, the results are, well, sweeter than honey!

Inner Inquiries for Journaling and Reflection

- What needs sweetening in my life right now? What needs healing?
- What stones, charms, or plant forms best symbolize where I am right now? What stones, charms, or plant forms would best symbolize where I want to be?

Personal Thank-You Scrolls

Sometimes, as we work with gratitude, we forget about addressing an entity with whom we're intimately connected: ourselves. And in the pursuit of a vocation or avocation, particularly one that's solitary, we may from time to time hunger for acknowledgment of the devotion and effort we're expending. When others take the time to do so, it can be motivating—but if outside appreciation is nowhere to be found, why not give it to ourselves?

Though it might seem at first blush to be self-indulgent, listing the gifts and talents that we bring to jobs and other enterprises—giving gratitude for them—can be a useful tool for staying the course. After all, if we're not appreciative of the unique qualities we bring to any project, why should we expect others to be? From a planning perspective, it's also a practical exercise to be aware of what we bring to the table, and what we don't; if we don't have a particular skill, that need can be supplemented by someone else.

There are many ways to approach this, to give gratitude to yourself. One way is to use the alphabet, and list twenty-six personal traits that you are grateful for, one for each letter. Another way is to use each letter of your full name to list qualities that you're grateful for. If you feel really inspired, you could start a scroll—just list qualities as they come to you, or list your achievements as you accomplish them—and keep the scroll rolled up where you can access it quickly when you need it, perhaps creating a special tie for it that includes charms with personal significance. If you really find it uncomfortable to do a practice like this, consider it a form of self-development. For as motivational expert John Demartini encourages us, "Whatever we think about and thank about, we bring about." That "whatever" includes our own personal attributes, so by thinking about ourselves as having particular gifts, and thanking the Universe that we have those gifts, we in effect strengthen and increase them.

Inner Inquiries for Journaling and Reflection

- Do I find it easy to acknowledge, appreciate, and be thankful for my gifts and talents? Why or why not?
- How could I incorporate a gratitude practice for my gifts and talents into my vocation or avocation? What kind of a difference might it make?

Looking at Patterns

"One of my gratitude practices is simply writing. Through writing, my thoughts become clear and I see more deeply inside a situation, and this leads to profoundest gratitude.

"When I wrote my book, *Follow the Yarn*, I set out to write a simple collection of knitting tips, along with some of the spicier pronouncements of my teacher, Ann Sokolowski, who was a real New York character. When she passed away suddenly nine months into our knitting class, the nature of the project changed. I found myself unable to continue in the vein I had begun. My soul seemed to insist that my personal story share space on the page along with Ann's. And so I wrote. To refuse to include my story would have meant to abandon the project altogether.

"The point that I want to make is that the more I shared of myself, the more my gratitude to Ann expanded and overflowed. By taking what I needed, what my soul had been starved for for many years, I was not taking anything away from Ann. Quite the opposite. By filling my cup, I discovered a newfound appreciation for the depths of Ann's greatness and the profound generosity of her invitation to me. For it was she who entrusted me with her story, she who authorized me to craft it exactly as I wished, and she who offered me the space to share my story.

"Only by allowing my soul what it needed could I fully experience the gift of what had been offered. In other words, the gifts may be there, the invitations might be there, but only if we accept them will we experience the incredible, perfect beauty of what is all around us, and to experience that beauty is to experience the deepest gratitude.

"So, receive! If we want to experience gratitude, we must open ourselves to receiving. We must pick up the pearls that lay strewn all around us. We must allow our innermost desires to surface and become part of our experience.

"Bringing this back to my gratitude practice, writing is the way that I allow who I am (and what I need) to surface. For others, their practice can be anything that puts them in touch with their authentic self, be it painting or meditating, or whatever.

"I just find it interesting to explore this kind of 'twist' to the idea of gratitude, whereby allowing ourselves to fully be who we are evokes the profoundest gratitude for ourselves, for life, and for our teachers, whoever or whatever they may be."

—REBA LINKER

One Thousand Dresses

If you've ever thought that you're too old to respond to a calling, then you need to hear the story of Lillian Weber. At the age of ninety-nine at the time of this writing, she has not only a passion but a quantifiable goal—to sew one thousand dresses for little girls in Africa by her hundredth birthday.

Lillian heard the call more than three years ago, and—feeling grateful for her dress-making gifts—decided to participate in a nonprofit project sponsored by Little Dresses of Africa, which on its website provides a simple pattern (made from a pillowcase!) that people can use to make dresses to send to African girls in need.

In an interview, Lillian expressed gratitude for the dexterity of her hands that allow her to still serve, commenting that sometimes she sings a song as she stitches! And Lillian is no sewing lightweight: She purposely uses a more demanding pattern, and a rainbow of various materials and embellishments such as lace and embroidered patches, to make each dress special—which of course makes the little girl receiving that dress feel special.

Lillian feels that it's part of her life mission, something that God has given to her to do—and she's grateful that by staying busy, she's also staying out of a nursing home. Will Lillian rest on her well-deserved laurels after finishing her thousandth dress? Not a chance, she says—she'll be sewing dresses for as long as she can.

Inner Inquiries for Journaling and Reflection

- What skill or skills do I have that could be used to pursue a calling to serve?
- What areas of the world, or areas of concern, call out to me? In what ways could I demonstrate my gratitude for all that I have through a service project?

"Gratitude should not be just a reaction to getting what you want, but an all-the-time gratitude, the kind where you notice the little things and where you constantly look for the good, even in unpleasant situations."

—MARELISA FABREGA

DIY: Sewing a Pillowcase Dress

If you, like Lillian, would like to sew dresses for Little Dresses for Africa (www.littledressesforafrica.org), or if there's another charitable organization you'd like to donate dresses to, here's the pattern from the Little Dresses for Africa website:

1. First, cut off the closed end of a pillowcase.

2. Fold the pillowcase in half lengthwise and cut armholes. Cut through all thicknesses, about 4 inches down and 2 inches in.

3. Fold down the top about ⅜ inch toward the inside of the pillowcase at the front and the back. Edgestitch to make a casing. Slide 6 inches of ¼-inch-wide elastic through to cause it to gather in the front. Repeat for the back.

4. Cut two 38-inch lengths of double-fold bias tape for the armholes. Fold each in half and stitch along the armholes, leaving extra at the top to tie the dress at the shoulders. Trim is optional.

Values Bracelets

As writer, editor, and artist Tonia Jenny writes, "On any given day it can seem as if we are adding nothing meaningful to the work we are doing, nor are we leaving those we work with feeling any better when we leave the workplace for the day than when we came in.

"It's easy for us to take our unique strengths for granted and to assume that 'little things' (which aren't actually little at all) that come easy to us also come as easily to everyone else. Guess what? Values such as humor, compassion, creative thinking, authenticity, and long-term thinking are but a few examples of things that are second nature to some of us, yet completely alien to the rest of us.

"On the flip side, it might feel as if we're being boastful when we share with others what we know to be our Divine gifts—the set of values that make us unique. But the truth is, the sole purpose of our gifts is to bring more love and light into the world through their use. The way our values combine, making us each into one beautiful being, makes each of us perfectly equipped to make a contribution no one else can! Not only are those we work with grateful to us for the values we bring to our work, but we should be grateful for them as well, for these values make it effortless for us to engage in a meaningful, positive, helpful way.

"When I started taking a serious look at my top core values, I began to feel good about my contribution to the world. Creating adornment that celebrates the qualities that make me unique is just one small but easy way for me to bring more meaning into daily life. And it's the meaningful details in our day-to-days that, by their very nature, celebrate gratitude."

Because Tonia feels so passionately about the need to explore and celebrate our personal values, she has created an exercise to discover them and a personalized bracelet pattern for us to be reminded of them. Tonia continues:

"So how does one drill down all the values they cherish to the super-powerful Top Five? Here's one fairly easy exercise that works every time. Without overthinking it, if you could have a fine meal and lovely conversation with any five individuals you can imagine (people you actually know, or don't know—real or fictional—it doesn't matter), who would be on that list? These are people you look up to and admire deeply. Now, jot down the characteristics you most admire about each. And here's the fun part: These things you value about these people are actually the same traits you hold yourself (or at the very least, hold great potential to nourish and strengthen). Compare the values across individuals. Do some values repeat? These are particularly strong in you. Look at the list as a whole and determine which five are most important to you—ones you couldn't live without—and you have your list of Top Five values!"

DIY: Crafting a Values Bracelet

Tonia, a skilled crafter, has generously included instructions for crafting a values bracelet below. Should you decide to take a simpler approach, the meaningfulness of this activity won't be lost; with this as with every other craft mentioned, the purpose is found in the process, not the final product!

Put three or four craft (popsicle) sticks into a pot and add several inches of water. (You'll only need one stick, but for this step, use a few because one or more may break.) Place the pot on the stove and bring the water to a boil. Leave the sticks boiling in the water for at least thirty minutes. Be sure to tend to the pot to make sure the water doesn't boil dry. After thirty minutes of boiling, remove the pot from the heat and leave the sticks in the hot water for an additional thirty minutes.

Remove a stick from the water and gently ease it into a curve until it is curved enough to put around the perimeter of the inside of an empty drinking glass. If it breaks, don't worry; just try again with another stick. Put as many sticks into glasses as you can manage. Leave the sticks in the glasses to dry completely.

Select the stick with the nicest shape for your bracelet. Using sturdy scissors, carefully cut off 3/4 inch from each end of the stick. Alternatively, this can be done with a fine saw, such as a jeweler's saw or small coping saw. Use sandpaper or a file to smooth the cut ends and round the sharp corners.

Approximately 1/8 inch from each end of the stick, drill a 1/8-inch hole, centered crosswise on the stick.

Using acrylic paint and a paintbrush, paint the wood in a color of your choice. Let the paint dry. For a distressed look, sand the paint a bit along the edges. Set this piece aside.

Cut a piece of shrink plastic (available at craft stores) to 1 by 2 1/4 inches. Cut off the corners using scissors or a hole punch.

Using a simple font that will be easy to trace, type the value you want to celebrate into a document on your computer. When printed, the word should be approximately 1/4 inch high. Print out the word and center the piece of shrink plastic lengthwise over the printout, then trace it with a fine-point permanent pen. Then, create a border by drawing a simple line close to the edge of the plastic on all sides.

With a 1/8-inch hole punch, punch a hole at each end of the word, approximately 1/8-inch from the edge of the plastic.

Working on a heat-resistant surface, shrink the plastic piece using a heat gun. Working quickly and carefully to avoid burning yourself, when the plastic is done shrinking, press it over the center of the painted craft stick while it's still warm, to give it a bit of a curve. Once the plastic is cool to the touch, paint the back of the plastic with a light-colored acrylic paint. If you get any paint on the sides of the plastic, don't worry; after it's dry, you can lightly sand or scrape it off. Set the plastic aside to dry.

Cut two ¾-inch-long pieces of elastic cord. Fold one piece in half and thread the two ends held together through the hole at one end of the plastic piece from back to front. Thread the ends through a crimp bead and, using crimping pliers, crimp the bead to secure the elastic. If you like, gently squeeze a crimp bead cover over the bead to finish it off. Repeat with the other piece of elastic for the hole on the other end of the plastic piece.

Drill two tiny holes centered crosswise on the craft stick, ⅝ inch and ¾ inch from each end, for a total of six holes (including the two you punched earlier). Be careful not to place the holes too close together, or you'll get one big hole! Choose two small buttons, a little larger than ¼ inch in diameter, and sew them onto the wood, using coat thread and sewing through the holes you just drilled. Tie off and trim the thread ends. Add a dot of glue to the knot.

Secure the plastic piece to the bracelet by looping the elastics around the buttons.

Determine how long you want your bracelet to be, and subtract 3 inches from that length. You will need a hook clasp to finish the bracelet. Measure the full length of your clasp (with the clasp hooked together) and add ¼ inch. Subtract this from the previous number and cut two pieces of silk cord to this length.

Fold one piece of silk cord in half and, holding the two ends together, crimp on a fold-over cord end. Thread the folded end through one end of the wood piece from front to back and then pull the cord end crimp through the loop to secure the silk cord. Repeat for the other piece of silk cord on the other end of the wood piece.

Using chain-nose pliers, attach the clasp to the cord ends using jump rings.

Your bracelet is complete! By wearing it, you're practicing a way to feel gratitude for the Divine gifts you've been given and to help yourself embrace them where you might tend to take them for granted.

Inner Inquiries for Journaling and Reflection

- What do I feel I contribute to the world right now?
- What would I like to contribute to the world in the future? What could I do that would represent my most cherished values?

> "Take full account of the excellencies which you possess, and in gratitude remember how you would hanker after them, if you had them not."
>
> —MARCUS AURELIUS

Professional Gratitude Journals

My foray into self-employment led to riches of a sort—definitely not monetary riches, but riches of experience and self-realization. I left the nonprofit world (or so I thought) in December 1999, so I could bring in the new millennium as a sole proprietor, the founder and principal of my own coaching and consulting business, which I named The New Story. Great name, great vision—the only problem was, I didn't have a clue as to how to be self-employed. My career up to that point had always involved being in an office and working with a team of other people—and all of a sudden the freedom I had craved also brought challenges. The challenges of getting work. The challenges of getting paid. The challenges of isolation, which I hadn't realized I would feel. So I know firsthand the roller-coaster ride that self-employment can be. It truly is a 24/7 endeavor, one in which it can be easy to feel less than optimistic, especially when you get your mail and the promised check has failed to arrive—*again*.

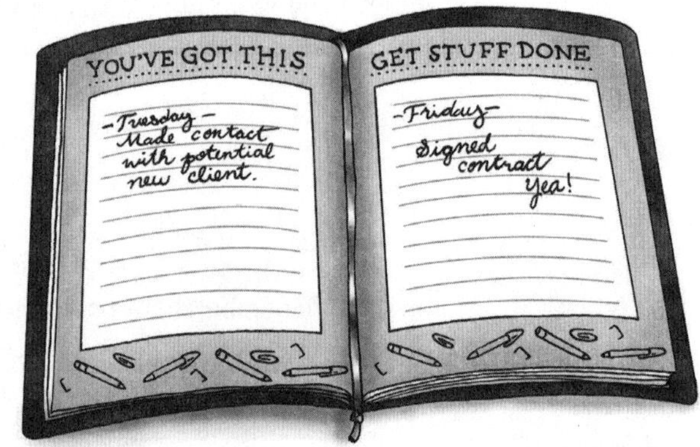

During that time, I knew that spiritually and emotionally, I needed to focus on all that *was* working well—that to keep my attention on what was lacking would only continue a cycle of depression and more lack. Because I was familiar with the concept of gratitude journals, I decided to keep one for my work. I vowed that I would make a point of listing every good thing that occurred with my business each day: a lead, an encouraging phone call, an idea that excited me, even a trip to an office-supply store that yielded the perfect filing container!

"God changes appearances every second. Blessed is the man who can recognize him in all his disguises. One moment he is a glass of fresh water, the next, your son bouncing on your knees or an enchanting woman, or perhaps merely a morning walk."

—NIKOS KAZANTZAKIS

Because I wanted to distinguish this gratitude journal from my personal one, I chose a periwinkle-blue suede one with a cut-out window in the front, into which I placed a circular, silver seal imprinted with my logo. Why periwinkle? Because I'll never forget the time almost two decades ago when someone complimented me on my periwinkle sweater, saying "I love that color; it's both calming and energizing." Since that was an effect that I hoped to achieve through my work, when I started my coaching and consulting business, periwinkle was the color I chose for my business collateral. There was something so pleasing about the softness of the suede journal, and the way I had personalized it, that it felt like an ongoing invitation to pick it up and list all the things I had to be grateful for in my business. (If you decide to start a professional gratitude journal, it can be powerful to choose one in the colors that represent your business or job to you—taken from a logo, perhaps, or a color that represents the feeling you want someone to experience through your work.)

While my path eventually—and somewhat surprisingly—led me into congregational ministry, I've kept my business identity—and that gratitude journal. It reminds me that no matter what is happening (or not happening) in my professional life, I can look for the goodness—and trust the process.

Inner Inquiries for Journaling and Reflection

- Whether I spend my days with others in a workplace, work as a sole proprietor, or am pursuing a calling, what are five things that I can be grateful for today with regard to my vocation or avocation?
- How might the tenor of my days change if I were to mindfully look for five things to be grateful for each day in the pursuit of my profession or passion?

> "The art of deep seeing makes gratitude possible. And it is the art of gratitude that makes joy possible. Isn't joy the art of God?"
>
> —ANN VOSKAMP

Chapter 6

Gratitude for Nature and Animals

Chapter 6:

Gratitude for Nature and Animals

"Any glimpse into the life of an animal quickens our own and makes it so much the larger and better in every way."

—JOHN MUIR

THERE ARE MANY THINGS THAT I HOPE TO INSTILL IN MY daughter, Chloe, as her mother and most obvious role model, and something I can give myself credit for right now was the conscious intention to make her a lover of animals. From the time Chloe joined our family, she lived with our elderly cat, Lani, who kept a wide swath of space around this noisy little newcomer until my daughter reached the age of about seven. Then, either too old or too tired to keep eluding our little girl, Lani surrendered—and she and Chloe enjoyed a close relationship until Lani died a month before her own twentieth birthday.

Now we have two new cats in our household, picked out as kittens at the SPCA and named by Chloe—Lulu and Lola, both black, both female, and (we think) from the same litter. Chloe has informed me that she is their mother and I am their grandmother; though I am not totally happy to be relegated to grandma status just yet, I am pleased that she feels so maternal toward our pets. During a Sunday school exercise in which the children made a collage of all they were grateful for, Chloe included images of animals, and both she and I have active Pinterest boards displaying photos of a vast array of species that run the gamut from the cute to the not-so-cute—mugs only a mother (or grandmother) could love.

I did not need to cultivate a love of nature in my girl; that, she was born with, and she has been an enthusiastic collector of sticks, stones, and other natural bits since she was tiny. Like many mothers, no doubt, I have been touched by her delight in picking what I would call a weed—and she would call a pretty flower.

What follows are some ideas for ways that you, too, can more fully appreciate and give gratitude for the natural delights in your life. We need to do what we can to remember that, in the words of Pamela Travers, "Magical things happen every day, if we allow it. Think of daylight, of the stars at night, a flower. A dandelion is a miracle."

Pet Memory Beads

Of all the animals I have ever loved—and there have been many—the one closest to my heart was the first cat that was ever my own, a black-and-cream ball of fluff named Luna. She entered my life when a friend of mine called to say that the night before, she had rescued a mewling three-month-old kitten out of a tree, during a rainstorm, on the night of a full moon. Would I take her?

The decision to say yes—a rather quick one—was one that illuminated my daily life with keen joy for almost nine years. A long-haired tortoiseshell cat with a plume-like tail and a dear heart-shaped face, Luna was my first living companion as an adult, and I doted on her.

Four years after I brought Luna home, a veterinary exam showed that her kidneys were malformed and she was, in fact, quite sick. I learned how to give her subcutaneous fluids with an IV-like setup; I learned, the hard way, where the emergency vet's office was.

I also pulled out all the spiritual stops I could think of: In addition to reading everything I could on her condition, I passed out pictures of Luna and asked pet-loving people to pray for her; I put holy water in her dish; I put a green healing crystal on her collar; I soothed and stroked and loved her, believing with all my heart that every purr I heard represented an internal endorphin surge that could strengthen her.

One night, after weeks of traumatic, touch-and-go incidents, I once again faced a decision regarding her care. Luna had vomited for the third time that day; it was after midnight; and because I'd been there before, I knew the routine: pack her up in the middle of the night, drive her to the twenty-four-hour emergency vet, watch them examine her on a cold, stainless-steel table, and then hand her over to them so they could put her in a cage and keep her under observation without me. I just couldn't do it to her.

I lined a box with soft material, put her in it, and placed it on the bed next to me. I decided to stay in gratitude: Sobbing, I thanked her for being with me, told her how much I loved her, and asked her to come back to me in another form if she wanted to. I lay down next to her, holding her little paw, which had tiny tufts of fur surrounding her mottled pink pads. With absolute, exhausting sadness, I tried to accept that it was time to let her go, while giving heartfelt thanks for the time I had had with her.

The next morning, through my fluttering, sleep-slowed eyelashes, I saw Luna. She was out of the box, sitting up, looking at me. My vet called her the "miracle cat." She stayed alive for another three and a half years, and I have no doubt that the gratitude I felt for her and to the Divine for every remaining moment I had with her had a healing effect on her.

When it was clearly time to say goodbye, when there were no more options left to try, I sat down on the couch on Luna's last night alive and made memory beads for my beloved kitty. I used the colors of her tortoiseshell fur—cream, brown, black—and included charms of significance: a tiger's-eye moon, a glass angel, two metal hearts intertwined, a little cat bell. Every time I look at them, I remember my little fur child and the joy she gave me, each bead and charm signifying the gratitude I felt and still feel—even thirteen years later—for having experienced such a deep love for a pet.

You, too, can express gratitude for a special pet by making a strand of pet memory beads, whether your animal companion is still with you or not. It's a tangible way of expressing thanks for the many intangible ways our cherished pets contribute to our lives—and can serve to mark precious memories of them when they're no longer with us.

Inner Inquiries for Journaling and Reflection

- Which pets in my life, past and present, have touched my life the most?
- How might I express gratitude for the special experience I've enjoyed with my pet?

"To speak gratitude is courteous and pleasant, to enact gratitude is generous and noble, but to live gratitude is Heaven."

—JOHANNES A. GAERTNER

Nature Photographs

In some ways, the beauty of nature is the quickest route to feelings of gratitude—perhaps because the awe we feel when looking at natural phenomena brings us back to gratitude, to the Divine, whether those phenomena are as large as pink-beige angles of giant granite boulders or as small as a delicate pale-blue spiral shell found at the beach. We know that what we witness in nature is something that we could not create ourselves; though we are all creators, only the ultimate Creator can make a flower.

Lauren Tober is an Australian clinical psychologist and yoga teacher who also founded an international Internet photography community. On the group's website, www.capturinggratitude.com, people from all over the world capture the large and small delights of their days—yellow, bite-sized tomatoes from the garden; a ringed moon in the night sky; the bluish-purple ombre hues of the Applachian Mountains. Lauren recalls, "Capturing Gratitude started out as an experiment. I was blessed with an iPhone for my birthday a few years ago, and hence found myself with a camera in my bag every day.

"Inspired by Brené Brown's work on gratitude and the research supporting its efficacy in changing lives, I'd begun including gratitude meditations in my yoga classes and counseling sessions, and started taking photographs of things I was grateful for every day. Straightaway, I noticed the positive effects of my gratitude practice. Happiness crept up on me. Honestly, I didn't expect the effects to be so immediate and so profound. I felt so blessed by everything in my life, and was able to find things to be grateful for, in even the challenges in daily life. I began sharing my gratitude photographs on my blog and on Facebook.

"My photographic gratitude experiment started inspiring others to take their own gratitude photographs, and in November 2012, Capturing Gratitude was born.

"Over two hundred gorgeous souls from all over the world joined us in taking photographs and sharing them online, and the sense of community and loving support was breathtaking.

"I have been so inspired by the life-changing power of the simple practice of gratitude that I'm on a mission to share it far and wide. Whether it's taking photographs or practicing in another way, gratitude changes lives. And by changing lives, it changes the world. We're making the world a better place. One grateful moment at a time."

Lauren created an e-book featuring interviews with contributors along with their photographs, as well as a thirty-day online course with ideas, inspiration, and prompts for using your camera to experience and share gratitude. The photos don't have to depict subjects from nature, though many of them do—they can be photographs of anything that causes you to feel grateful. So many sights, sounds, and people move through the course of our days; why not "collect" one or two with your cell-phone camera to remind you of the bounty of your blessings?

> "We often take for granted the very things that most deserve our gratitude."
>
> —CYNTHIA OZICK

Inner Inquiries for Journaling and Reflection

- What aspects of nature might you be passing by each day without taking the time to really look at them?
- What aspects of nature give you the most pleasure? What do you not resonate with? Reflect on what makes the difference to you.

"What if you gave someone a gift, and they neglected to thank you for it—would you be likely to give them another? Life is the same way. In order to attract more of the blessings that life has to offer, you must truly appreciate what you already have."

—RALPH MARSTON

Blessing Trees

I still have it, though it is dry and fragile with age: a small, heart-shaped leaf on which is written "blessings to maggie" in teeny, fairylike, fine-line letters. It originally accompanied a gift given to me by my friend Susan; little did she know that this leaf "card" would be as meaningful to me as what came wrapped up in patterned paper and bow.

Leaves, and the trees they fall from, are rife with metaphor when it comes to gratitude. No wonder poet E. E. Cummings chose, in his elegiac poem "i thank You God," to celebrate both of them.

Starting in ancient times, trees have both been worshipped and have been the vehicle for worship, as people around the world, in various faith traditions and for various reasons, have gathered around these majestic spires with which we share the earth. And still, around the globe, in locales as diverse as Japan, Scotland, and Siberia, people gather around trees to express their gratitude or hang their prayers. Modern-day manufacturers have noted this practice and made the great outdoors unnecessary by making metal prayer trees small enough for a tabletop, onto which you can fasten your written wishes.

Given this primal, almost ancestral love of trees that most human beings share, creating a personal or family "blessing tree" is a wonderful way to stay mindful to all we have to be grateful for. Whether your indoor tree is real or silk, its branches can be used as a place to tie rolled-up paper missives of prayer and thanksgiving.

Should you decide to work with a blessing tree as a gratitude practice, first decide whether you want to use the tree on particular occasions or leave it up year-round. Then reflect on these questions: scale (small or large?), placement (indoors or outdoors?), participants (individual or family/community?), intention (to hang prayers or to hang gratitudes?). Once you've decided on these things, your practice can begin. No matter how you use your tree, remember that, as Martin Luther so poetically said, "God writes the Gospel not in the Bible alone, but also on trees, and in the flowers and clouds and stars."

Inner Inquiries for Journaling and Reflection

- What phase of growth best represents the emotional season of life I feel myself in right now—a green sapling, just beginning to bud? A mighty maple, resplendent with a golden cape of autumn leaves? A stark birch tree, barren and cold to the touch?
- If I were writing a thank-you poem to God, as E. E. Cummings did, what would I include in my list of things to be grateful for?

> "Gratitude promotes healing, harmony, peace, and joy. It encourages forgiveness, patience, and goodwill. It is a path that opens the opportunity for you to act on the good in your life."
>
> —MARY BETH SAMMONS

Gratitude Rocks

In the movie *The Secret*, business coach Lee Brower talks about his practice of using a gratitude rock, which people all over the world have adopted thanks to the phenomenal success of that movie and the book of the same name by Rhonda Byrne. He tells of how, during a challenging time in his life, he found a rock near his home and decided to keep it in his pocket during the day; every time he touched it, he would remember to think of something he was grateful for. At night, he would empty his pockets and place his rock on the dresser; in the morning, he would put the rock back into his pocket and start the process again.

Once, he remembers, a man from South Africa saw the rock fall out of his pocket and asked Brower what it was. Brower explained, and a number of months later he received an email from the man, whose son was very ill. He asked if Brower could send him some gratitude rocks, which Brower did, picking out special ones from a nearby stream. Happily, the man's son got well—and the father wrote Brower that people in that community had sold more than one thousand gratitude rocks at ten dollars each and given the money to charity!

In a follow-up book to *The Secret*, called *The Magic*—which focuses entirely on the power of gratitude—author Rhonda Byrne expanded this practice. She suggests putting your gratitude rock on your nightstand, and before you go to sleep, holding it in your hand and thinking of the very best thing that happened to you that day, then saying "thank you."

If you'd like to work with a gratitude rock, have fun with the process of selecting just the right one. Perhaps take a nature walk in a favorite place and notice what calls to you. Begin with gratitude that Mother Earth provides a treasure trove of possible rocks to choose from; delight in the differing shapes and shades as you choose the perfect one.

Whether you keep it in your purse or pocket to touch during your waking hours or keep it by your bed to acknowledge the highlight of the day—or both—using a gratitude rock is a simple, free, and powerful practice. You might even say that gratitude rocks!

Inner Inquiries for Journaling and Reflection

- Did I have a rock collection as a child? Or do I already have a stone or rock that has significance to me? What do its shape, color, or the location where I found it symbolize to me?
- Do I know the folkloric symbolism that is ascribed to certain rocks, minerals, and gems? How might I begin to work with some of these associations?

Common Associations for Stones and Gemstones

AMAZONITE: Balances emotions, gives stamina, enhances communication in relationships

AMETHYST: Enhances spiritual awareness, attracts love and good luck, protects against inebriation and poison

AVENTURINE: Brings opportunity and luck; helps with anxiety and retaining energy, as well as with decision-making

BLUE LACE AGATE: Enhances spiritual inspiration, calms and uplifts thoughts, eliminates negativity and anger

CARNELIAN: Clears negative energy, helps develop a sense of humor, calms the temper, awakens inner talents and creativity

CITRINE: Creates clarity and self-esteem, enhances creativity and optimism, stimulates abundance

FLUORITE: Eases change and brings strength and protection during transition, stabilizes energy, helps to bring order by neutralizing negative emotions

FOSSIL: Helps to release limiting beliefs and old programming, increases business accomplishments

GARNET: Revitalizes and balances energy, inspires devotion and love, clears negative energy, brings success in business

HEMATITE: Enhances memory and concentration, deflects negativity, increases intuition

JASPER: Helps to balance and unite physical and spiritual energy, provides protection against negativity

LABRADORITE: Supports originality and uniqueness, stimulates imagination and enthusiasm

LAPIS LAZULI: Assists with spiritual growth, supports clarity, helps to organize daily activities, offers protection

MALACHITE: Aids in releasing negative emotional experiences, increases intuition, stimulates loyalty in friendship and love, brings success in business

ROSE QUARTZ: Soothes, comforts, and heals; brings peace and calm to relationships; opens the heart to love

TIGER'S EYE: Helps to think more clearly and to organize, calms turmoil, encourages optimism and enthusiasm for life, brings a feeling of oneness

TURQUOISE: Dispels negative energy, protects, encourages creativity, brings peace of mind, symbolizes friendship, brings connection to Spirit

"How delightful is the company of generous people, who overlook trifles and keep their minds instinctively fixed on whatever is good and positive in the world about them."

—ANNE SOPHIE SWETCHINE

Flower Mandalas

I first learned about flower mandalas from the twenty-first-century virtual filing system known as Pinterest; having started a board dedicated to mandalas, the ancient spiritual artworks of Hinduism and Buddhism that depict a circle (*mandala* is the Sanskrit word for "circle") with intricate patterns inside upon which to meditate, I was intrigued when photographs of mandalas made of flower petals, pods, seeds, and other natural elements came up during a search.

I learned that this practice is a nod to *rangoli*, a type of folk art from India in which patterns (not necessarily circular) are created on the ground from flower petals or colored rice, sand, or flour, usually during an Indian festival period such as Diwali. These patterns can be made with wet or dry ingredients; their purpose is simply decoration, though they are also believed to be good luck.

In these beautiful, multicolored images, I saw echoes of the British artist Andy Goldsworthy, who uses materials from nature—ranging from pine needles to ice—to fashion organic sculptures that are meant to be transient, as nature is; as indeed life is. Doing more research, I discovered that the person who most probably was the creator of many of these beautiful mandalas I was seeing on the Internet is an Arizona artist named Kathy Klein, who calls her creations "danmalas," from Sanskrit words that together mean "the giving of flower circles."

As her website explains, Kathy begins her process in a devotional meditative state, and she sees her creations as "reflections of the inexpressible, a gesture which points towards life's abundance, an unspoken verse of Love. The danmalas remind us all to listen to the unheard voice of nature, creation, and the eternal mystery."

Because of their beauty and fragrance, creating a flower mandala is indeed a creative act of gratitude. Try exploring flower mandalas as a gratitude practice—and see what blooms in your heart.

Inner Inquiries for Journaling and Reflection

- What is being seeded in me? What is blooming in me?
- What do I want to be seeded in me? What do I want to be blooming in me?

Meanings of Flowers

The following lists the positive associations for some common flowers whose petals might find their way into your flower mandala.

CARNATIONS symbolize beauty; specifically, red carnations symbolize love, pink carnations symbolize the love of a woman or a mother, and white carnations symbolize innocence and pure love.

CHRYSANTHEMUMS symbolize fidelity, joy, long life, and optimism. Specifically, red chrysanthemums symbolize love, and white chrysanthemums symbolize truth and loyalty.

DAISIES symbolize innocence, purity, and loyal love.

GERBERA DAISIES symbolize cheerfulness.

HYDRANGEAS symbolize heartfelt emotions and can express gratitude for being understood.

LILACS symbolize youthful innocence and confidence. Specifically, white lilacs symbolize humility and innocence, and purple lilacs symbolize first love.

QUEEN ANNE'S LACE symbolizes a haven or sanctuary.

ROSES symbolize love. Their different colors signify love of various forms.

STATICE symbolizes remembrance, sympathy, and success.

SUNFLOWERS symbolize adoration, dedicated love, and pure thoughts.

SWEET PEAS symbolize bliss and pleasure; they also symbolize leavetaking after a good time.

"Look closely and you will find that people are happy because they are grateful. The opposite of gratefulness is just taking everything for granted."

—BROTHER DAVID STEINDL-RAST

Chapter 7

Gratitude for Opportunities and Possibilities

Chapter 7:

Gratitude for Opportunities and Possibilities

"Your diamonds are not in far distant mountains or in yonder seas; they are in your own backyard, if you but dig for them."

—RUSSELL H. CONWELL

THERE IS A CURIOUS PARADOX THAT THE STUDY OF GRATITUDE uncovers: The less we think we have, the less we actually have—and the more we think we have, the more we seem to attract. Though this is of course a subtle mind shift of the classic "Is the glass half-full or half-empty?" variety, practitioners of gratitude have found that indeed, their cups runneth over when they focus on the fullness they see.

Perhaps no arena is as crucial for self-development as that of seeing opportunities and possibilities for our lives. Scripture says that "where there is no vision, the people perish," and experience bears that out—how can we experience the totality of possibilities for our lives when we fail to see the opportunities all around us? That is why rags-to-riches stories are so compelling: because someone had the vision to see beyond their circumstances and dream a better dream. It is why we get so inspired when we hear a story like Oprah Winfrey's. You may think you already know it, but listen to it again: Born to an unwed teenage mother, she spent her earliest years on her grandmother's farm in Mississippi; her grandmother taught her to read by the age of three. When she was six, she moved to Milwaukee to live with her mother, who worked as a maid—and from the ages of nine to thirteen, she was molested by male relatives and a family "friend" during the time when her mother was out of the apartment working. At fourteen, Oprah moved out of that house to be on her own, but after giving birth to a baby boy who died as an infant, she went to live with her father in Nashville.

From that point on the trajectory of her life started to change. Oprah's father set strict standards for her behavior, and she started flourishing in school, becoming an honors student and later winning a scholarship to Tennessee State University and majoring in speech communications and performing arts. She signed on with a local television station as a reporter and anchor, and we know the rest: She is now a media mogul known around the globe with an honorary degree from Harvard and a Presidential Medal of Freedom, and is the first black woman billionaire in world history, with—at the time I am writing this—a net worth of $3 billion.

Hearing a story like that, about someone who rose from beginnings of abject poverty and abuse to accomplish things that literally no one has ever done before, we can do well to also believe in the possibilities for our own lives. We can do well to heed the words of Oprah herself: "I started out giving thanks for small things, and the more thankful

I became, the more my bounty increased. That's because what you focus on expands, and when you focus on the goodness in your life, you create more of it. Opportunities, relationships, even money flowed my way when I learned to be grateful no matter what happened in my life."

"There are only two ways to live your life. One is as though nothing is a miracle. The other is as if everything is."

—ALBERT EINSTEIN

Affirmation Decks

If you're reading this book, you already know—or soon will know—the joy of creating something that is personally meaningful to you, something that taps your creative spirit and draws you closer to Spirit, however you define that. Although using a ready-made reflection or divination deck can be a powerful practice for self-exploration, there is nothing like creating one yourself using the images, words, colors, and symbols that speak most deeply to you.

Thanks to the ever-expanding crafting movement, there are many possibilities for doing this. If working on a smaller scale appeals to you, you can find ready-made ATCs (Artist Trading Cards) available in most craft stores. If you like a traditional playing-card size, you could buy an inexpensive deck of playing cards and modify the cards with your own images. For less traditional sizes, you could visit a hardware store and pick up paint chips—many of them now come in palm-sized squares that could also be embellished. And if you'd like a larger size still, you can buy precut cards measuring 8 x 5 inches used for a process called SoulCollage on the SoulCollage website (www.soulcollage.com).

To make your affirmation deck, first consider what you'd like to use it for: to affirm that which you'd like to see in your life? Or to remind yourself of what you already have? It could be a very meaningful process to collage images that remind you of your abundant blessings; perhaps you could make "suits" around different categories of your life that you're grateful for: People, Places, Things, Personal Attributes, and Experiences.

Having your own personalized affirmation deck can help you to be more present to the Divine language that is always being spoken all around us. And, as spiritual writer and leader Ernest Holmes once wrote, “When we recognize the Divine Presence everywhere, then we know that it responds to us and that there is a Law of God, a Law of Love, forever giving of itself to us.”

Inner Inquiries for Journaling and Reflection:

- Do I have a deck that I already use on a regular basis when I want more clarity about something happening in my life? What appeals to me about it—its size, its colors, its symbols, its images?
- How could I bring my affirmation deck into my daily spiritual practice, so that gratitude stays before me as a focus?

Blessing Sachets

The word *sachet* comes from a French word meaning "little bag," and its definition, according to Dictionary.com, is "a small bag, case, or pad containing aromatic powder, flower parts, or the like." And it's that "like" part that can turn a regular sachet into a fragrant celebration of gratitude.

Historically, sachets have an interesting history. They were worn during the Han dynasty by both men and women, though with time the habit of wearing scented sachets fell out of favor with men. Sachets were later used as love tokens, and, filled with herbs conducive to sleepiness, they have also been known through the centuries as "dream pillows."

Sachets can be any size and shape, though they are most usually squares of approximately three to four inches. Because of their traditional simple shape, they are easy to make, and blessing sachets can be made as gifts to give others, to let them know what a treasure they are in your life. As a gratitude practice, they also could be made as affirmations for a particular dream or goal as you give thanks in advance—placing inside them charms, written prayers, photos, herbs, and flowers that represent the dream your little sachet square holds.

Whatever purpose you decide on for your blessing sachet, the making of it holds the possibility of being a prayer. Indeed, perhaps taking our cue from the mystic poet Rumi, who wrote that he wanted to be thankful for even the small occurrences of life, we can use our sachet to remind us of the many elements, large and small, that give our lives such delectable spice.

Inner Inquiries for Journaling and Reflection

- Who or what provides the beautiful "fragrance" in my life? What people or things perfume my life through their blessings?
- What dream or goal would I like to see grow?

> "I am thankful before You,
> Living and Sustaining Ruler,
> Who returned my soul to me with mercy,
> Your faithfulness is great."
>
> —MODEH ANI (JEWISH MORNING PRAYER)

Common Meanings of Herbs

ALLSPICE: good luck, good fortune

BASIL: love, good wishes

BAY LEAF: achievement and fame

CHIVES: usefulness

CINNAMON: success, power

CUMIN: fidelity

CURRY: protection

DILL: good cheer; survival in the face of difficult odds

EUCALYPTUS: healing

GARLIC: protection against theft

GINGER ROOT: money, success, power

GRAPEFRUIT PEEL: energy

IVY: fidelity and marriage, friendship, wedded love

JUNIPER/JUNIPER BERRIES: protection

MINT: refreshment, virtue

PARSLEY: merriment, lack of bitterness

PEPPERMINT: cordiality, warmth of feeling

POPPY SEED: fertility

ROSEMARY: remembrance

SAGE: long life, wisdom, esteem

SANDALWOOD: spirituality

SESAME: money

SPEARMINT: warmth of sentiment

STAR ANISE: luck; also believed to increase psychic powers

TARRAGON: a lasting involvement

THYME: daring, activity, courage

WHEAT: prosperity

(See also the list of common flower meanings on page 136 and the list of despacho ingredient meanings on page 172.)

"Take one thing with another, and the world is a pretty good sort of world, and it is our duty to make the best of it, and be grateful."

—BENJAMIN FRANKLIN

Visual Gratitude Journals

Jeniffer Hutchins knows all about the connection between creativity and spirituality; this connection is something she has pursued both individually and as an instructor. Keeping a visual journal—a journal in which images are as important as, if not more important than, words—is her way of keeping a gratitude journal that nourishes her.

"I absolutely use my visual journal as an act of gratitude," Jeniffer says. "I consider working in my journal a form of prayer. For me, prayer and gratitude are interconnected. When I sit down to my journal, I first set an intention for my session. My intention may be to focus on a project I am working on, to work through a challenge I am facing, or to center myself after a busy day. Sometimes I begin working in my journal by letting my thoughts ramble out in inky letters. Other times I use art materials such as paint, colored pencils, or even crayons to fill my blank page with color. This first step is *release*. It is a way I release my thoughts, emotions, and built-up energy around the situation.

"Once I release, my mind becomes more calm and focused. Then I move on to the next step of my journaling process, *receptivity*. I tune in to the inner answers that begin to emerge. I capture those thoughts in words, colors, and imagery. This is tapping the Source, the Light, the Wisdom within me.

"The final step is gratitude. It is expressing immense thanks for receiving the answers I needed and the knowing that they have been available to me all along. These thoughts of gratitude may express themselves through words, drawings, or collage. Often I simply write the words 'Thank you' directly on my journal page. Other times, I complete my prayer-filled journal page by turning deeper within and thanking my Source, thanking God for all the blessings in my life.

"Keeping an art journal is just one way that I practice gratitude through creative expression," Jeniffer says. "I believe all forms of artistic expression allow us the opportunity to craft gratitude. Through artistic expression I have come to better understand myself and my connection to the creative Spirit that lives in us all. For me, art is an expression of love, of joy, and of deep gratitude."

Jeniffer finds inspiration for her visual journal in all kinds of places: "I am often inspired by places where man has trodden lightly in nature: old farmhouses and barns; long, winding country roads; a nature path through a field of wildflowers; a rising sun over a pier. There are moments when being in these places literally takes my breath away. I am filled with a lightness, with a sense of joy, simplicity, and peace. I want to capture those moments, to make them last, and to share that sensation with others. That is why I create. Whether I am painting a rural landscape, writing an article on faith, or creating a collage in my journal, art is a means by which I express myself from my heart. My artwork becomes a prayer of gratitude for the beauty I see, the joy I feel, and the inspiration I have received."

To begin your own practice with a visual gratitude journal, buy a sketchbook and some colored pencils and markers and use these tools as your "camera" as you walk through your days. Notice what brings you gratitude, and whether consciously looking for things to be grateful for brings more of them your way. Remember that this is not about making something; it is about expressing something. It is about expressing gratitude to your Maker (however you define that) for the many blessings of your day—and life.

Inner Inquiries for Journaling and Reflection

- Do I have an outlet for my creative expression? How could I use a visual journal to capture the gratitude I feel?
- What does happiness mean to me?

> "When you arise in the morning, give thanks for the food and for the joy of living. If you see no reason for giving thanks, the fault lies only in yourself."
>
> —CHIEF TECUMSEH

Crafting a Gratitude Practice

"When we create with a grateful heart, we invite more opportunities for joy and happiness into our lives. Here is a simple activity you can do as a practice for creating gratitude. In a journal or on a loose-leaf sheet of paper, write the words 'Happiness is.' Now fill the page with all you can think of to complete the phrase. What makes you feel happy? What brings you joy? You may use words, scribble little pictures, or cut images out of a magazine. The only rule is to fill the whole page.

"Take time to reflect on your creation. Let your gratitude pour forth as you notice how many things on your page are already in your life. Invite even more happiness into your life by giving thanks for the opportunity to reflect on each of the items."

—JENIFFER HUTCHINS

Zentangle® Drawings

Though the name may not yet mean anything to you, you have probably seen them: black ink drawings on white paper, of every conceivable shape and subject, embellished with various levels of patterned intricacy. While they look like complex drawings, in fact, they're also a form of meditation that adherents say can be highly beneficial in multiple arenas of mind, body, and spirit.

On a blog devoted to this drawing method, which carries the registered-trademark name of Zentangle (found at www.zentangle.com), it is described this way: "Zentangle is an easy-to-learn, relaxing, and fun way to create beautiful images by drawing structured patterns." The technique was created by Rick Roberts and Maria Thomas, who have trademarked the process. They explain their motivation: "We believe that life is an art form and that the Zentangle method is an elegant metaphor for deliberate artistry in life."

Tess Carlson Imobersteg is a Zentangle practitioner and teacher. She explains the process further: "Zentangle is an art process used for many different purposes, including relieving stress, increasing creativity and focus, as an approach to mindfulness, as a way to change perspective, and much more." Tess adds, "My favorite part of Zentangle classes is to see beginning students who declare they can't 'do' art, relax, focus, and with wonder create Zentangle drawings as beautiful as those of anyone else in the class."

And how could Zentangle be used as a gratitude practice? "Gratitude is a basic tenet in preparing for a Zentangle session," Tess explains. "The Zentangle process is, in part, a small personal ceremony or ritual. Ceremonies and rituals are familiar and comforting parts of our lives. One aspect of a ceremony is that when you begin, you are drawn into a familiar state of mind.

"There are several steps in the Zentangle process, and the very first is to take a few deep breaths and give yourself several moments to feel gratitude and appreciation. This is one of my favorite parts of teaching Zentangle and one I emphasize.

"Thinking about what we are personally grateful for centers us, puts the mind at peace, helps us to shed stress, and allows us to open our minds creatively. These are some of the goals of Zentangle. I am presently working on a journal that has gratitude as a theme."

Though with a quick Internet search you can find instructions for how to do Zentangle, it is recommended that you either buy a learning kit (available on the Zentangle website) or work with a certified instructor like Tess. Zentangle is powerful as a gratitude practice because the process begins and ends in gratitude; as the Zentangle website explains, "Gratitude is our foundation. It also informs our product design and our teaching method. Whether it's appreciating the texture of these wonderful paper tiles, becoming aware of the patterned beauty around us, or being grateful for the opportunity to put pen to paper, we always return to gratitude."

Inner Inquiries for Journaling and Reflection

- What in my life feels as if it's progressing in a linear fashion, from Point A to Point B? What feels like it's rambling, swerving, going every which way?
- What in my life seems "black and white"? Where in my life are there a lot of gray areas?

"I find that the more willing I am to be grateful for the small things in life, the bigger stuff just seems to show up from unexpected sources, and I am constantly looking forward to each day with all the surprises that keep coming my way!"

—LOUISE L. HAY

Gratitude Dream Catchers

Though once solely the practice of certain Native American tribes, dream catchers have become a part of contemporary Western culture—the term "dream catcher" has been used in book and movie titles, and the dream catcher has gone from something hung over one's bed to a popular motif on clothing, jewelry, and even tattoos.

You've doubtless seen them, even if you didn't know what they were called: round hoops covered with leather or ribbon that contain a web of string inside, usually adorned with hanging strands of beads and feathers. The original intent of the Native American dream catcher was literally to catch bad dreams—a dream catcher hanging above one's sleeping area, it was believed, would filter out all bad dreams and allow only positive images and thoughts to enter one's mind. With the rising of the sun, all the negativity would disappear, and one would be left with only the good on which to dwell.

This original intent is an interesting one to think of in terms of crafting gratitude, because often we fail to see all the good that surrounds us due to our focus on the negative, the "bad dreams" of our lives. Why not create a gratitude dream catcher to filter out the negative and free us to focus on the good?

A quick Internet search will show you many possible ways to approach your dream catcher—there's even a version for kids to make, using a paper plate with the center removed. Depending on the desired purpose of your dream catcher and your level of technical expertise, you can make this gratitude practice as simple or complex as you wish; if you want to replicate the original ways in which dream catchers were made, there are even instructions available for using branches, soaking them first to make them soft enough to form a hoop.

No matter how you choose to use your gratitude dream catcher, let it be a symbol to remind you that, as one anonymous philosopher put it, "A good life is when you smile often, dream big, laugh a lot, and realize how blessed you are for what you have."

Inner Inquiries for Journaling and Reflection

* What do I need to filter out of my life? What are the thoughts or habits that keep me dwelling on the negative?
* What are the dreams that I want to let through? What would make me feel excited and happy to be alive upon awakening each day?

DIY: Crafting a Gratitude Dream Catcher

Though there are many ways to construct a dream catcher, ranging from simple to complex (depending on the materials you use), here is one to try:

Using a hot glue gun, attach the end of a piece of ribbon or leather cord to a metal craft hoop of whatever size you desire. Wrap the leather or ribbon tightly around the hoop so that no metal shows. Once the hoop has been completely covered, affix the other end of the ribbon or cord to the hoop with the hot glue gun.

Then, take a lighter-weight threading material (this could be thread, yarn, a thin leather cord, or twine) and tie a knot to attach one end of it to your hoop. Stretch a length of cord from the knot to another point on the hoop, wrap it around the outside of the hoop, and repeat at equal distances until the cord has been wrapped around the hoop at five to eight points, forming the outside of a star pattern. Then, beginning again where you started, take your threading material and do the same thing again—but now wrap it around the middle of the lengths of thread you just attached to the hoop, which will create a new level of webbing. Continue until you have only a small opening in the middle, pulling your thread tightly as you make your webbing. When you are happy with the way the web looks, tie a tight knot (adding a bead or charm if you like) and trim off the excess.

All that remains now is to embellish your dream catcher. You can attach a loop at the top to hang it from, then create strands that will dangle from the bottom, using feathers, ribbons, charms, or beads.

Chapter 8

GRATITUDE FOR THE DIVINE

Chapter 8:

GRATITUDE FOR THE DIVINE

"Gratitude is the intention to count your blessings every day, every minute, while avoiding, whenever possible, the belief that you need or deserve different circumstances."

—TIMOTHY RAY MILLER

OUR PRACTICE OF CRAFTING GRATITUDE ENDS HERE, BUT IT begins here too—the source of all that we have to be grateful for is, in fact, our Source. No matter what your circumstances currently are, chances are that if you are reading this book, you have been gifted with more than the majority of the world's inhabitants and are very blessed indeed.

If you doubt those words, an infographic circulating on the Internet gives us this perspective: "If you have food in your fridge, clothes on your back, a roof over your head, and a place to sleep, you are richer than 75 percent of the world. If you have money in the bank, your wallet, and some spare change, you are among the top 8 percent of the world's wealthy. If you woke up this morning with more health than illness, you are more blessed than the million people who will not survive this week. If you have never experienced the danger of battle, the agony of imprisonment or torture, or the horrible pangs of starvation, you are luckier than 500 million people alive and suffering."

How we choose to react to information like that can say a lot about how we are living our lives. Does it mean that God, Creator, the Universe doesn't care about those people who don't have what we have? No, of course not. Does it mean that maybe, just maybe, we might want to stop dwelling on what we don't have and start expressing gratitude to the Divine for all that we have? Unequivocally, yes. And if it inspires us to use our prosperity to help those who don't have as much, so much the better. For in the end, giving back a measure of what we ourselves have been given is the ultimate way of expressing thanks. As John F. Kennedy so wisely reminded us, "As we express our gratitude, we must never forget that the highest appreciation is not to utter words, but to live by them."

"Sometimes just giving thanks for the mystery of it all brings everything and everyone closer, the way suction pulls streams of water together. So take a chance and openly give thanks, even if you're not sure what for, and feel the plenitude of all that is living brush up against your heart."

—MARK NEPO

Gratitude Bracelets

I LOOK AT THE GRATITUDE BRACELET THAT WAS GIVEN TO ME by my friend and fellow Unity minister Lauren McLaughlin, and as I finger the beads, I feel waves of gratitude for differing things: for the beauty of the beads, which always captivate my attention; for the gift of sight, which allows me to appreciate the pale-green glass painted with a subtle white squiggle; for the simplicity and helpfulness of the practice, which is detailed below; for the gift of the bracelet's maker, an interesting and inspiring author and minister. Lauren explains how she began to make these beautiful gratitude bracelets:

"For about five years, I did most of my ministry through facilitating Gratefulness Retreats. Gratitude in all its forms became my signature teaching, and I developed a number of tools to help people establish the habit of expressing gratitude—not just by writing five lines at the end of the day, but by expressing gratitude spontaneously throughout the day. One of the tools I created was a gratitude bracelet, a simple beaded bracelet with ten principal etched-glass beads, which my students could use any time they had a moment of waiting—in a grocery store or bank line, while they were on hold on the telephone, while waiting for a meal to be served in a restaurant or for an appointment to start—and, because they worked by the sense of touch, even as they were waiting to fall asleep.

"The instructions for using the bracelet are to place your fingers on the one bigger, 'odd' separator bead to mark the beginning of the practice, and then to run your fingers around the glass beads, expressing either ten things to be grateful for in the moment or ten aspects to be grateful for about one thing. For example: my husband, my children, my dog, my home, my parents, my boss, my coworkers, my car, my health, and my bank account would be examples of ten separate things; or my car—because it provides me with shelter, movement, freedom, and the ability to do my work, run my errands, carry my friends from place to place, visit my parents, take my dog to the park, get to and from work, or see a sunset—that would be a way to use it to express ten aspects of a single blessing.

"Each student at one of my seminars received a bracelet as a gift and signed a pledge to use it at least once a day for ninety days. I got dozens of notes back from students saying they used it when they were waiting for all sorts of things, but also when they were anxious about things, like flying; when they were filled with joy; when they were bored or annoyed with someone. One woman even sent a picture of herself on the ninetieth day, sitting on the ground under the Eiffel Tower, expressing gratitude for the trip that had manifested for her during the ninety days! Of course I also reminded them that if they didn't have their bracelet with them, they could always use their ten fingers to perform the same gratitude exercise. Gratitude is one of the great spiritual practices that is always free and can always be performed by anyone, anywhere, anytime.

"An interesting side effect for me was that as I was making the bracelets, they also became a spiritual exercise for me," Lauren says. "I would bless the beads first, then the bracelets; and then the people who would receive the bracelets also blessed me, enormously. And making them for other reasons has also been a huge blessing. One woman commissioned me to make sixty to give away in an independent/assisted living facility where she worked, and she said residents just loved them. Some even used them together, as kind of a group activity. The overall attitude in the facility rose by noticeable notches.

"I continue to make them as gifts and will sell some if anyone wants them, although that's not my primary goal—and I am seldom without one myself. I'm not a patient waiter, so my bracelet helps to tone down my stress level. They make a great gift for someone who is ill or hospitalized, too, because they offer hope and shift attention from what is wrong to what is right in any given moment."

If you don't have a means for literally counting your blessings, a gratitude bracelet makes an easy and effective one. Because you wear it, it invites the practice every time you see or feel it—and wise people like Lauren know that the more we practice gratitude, the more we have to be grateful for.

Inner Inquiries for Journaling and Reflection

- Do I have a practice for noting ten things to be grateful for each day?
- Am I able to list ten things I receive from every one thing that I am grateful for?

Book of Hours

The practice of using a book of hours dates back to the Middle Ages, although more contemporary ones exist, such as one written by twentieth-century Trappist monk Thomas Merton. In these medieval prayer books, days were divided into eight segments, and different prayers and verses of scripture would be read during each passage of the day. There were *matins*, said during the hours before dawn; *lauds*, said at dawn; *prime*, mid-morning; *terce*, late morning; *sext*, noon; *none*, mid-afternoon; *vespers*, sundown; and *compline*, late evening. Generally speaking, these segments of the day traced the chronology of events from the life of the Virgin Mary; *prime* or mid-morning, for example, represented the birth of the Christ child.

These books were originally used in monasteries and laid open for monks to read from at the appropriate time. Later, smaller, portable prayer books were produced for the wealthy, featuring beautiful illuminated paintings embellished with silver and gold leaf. Usually each section of prayers had an accompanying illustration whose subject would help deepen the reader's contemplation and understanding.

While eight times a day may be ambitious, what a lovely way to consider offering praise to the Divine—the praise, as noted by editor Kathleen Deignan in the introduction to *A Book of Hours* by Thomas Merton, that "has ever been the preoccupation of those who live in vital awareness of a universe resplendent with mystery."

Praising the Divine, giving gratitude for our blessings eight times a day, would radically shift our experience of life. And though it may be difficult to schedule that into the course of every day, creating one's own personal book of hours is a wonderful start.

As the monks who created illuminations did, consider finding prayers, quotations, or images to mark each of those eight segments of the day—or use a lesser number, if that helps (especially for those of us who aren't used to rising in the wee hours before dawn!). What are you most grateful for at dawn? At midday? In the late evening? Find or create an image to mark each section of your book of hours, something that will help you to contemplate the blessings of that particular period of time—and watch your hours become very blessed indeed.

Inner Inquiries for Journaling and Reflection

- At what time of day am I usually the most grateful? What makes that time more conducive for feeling or expressing gratitude?
- How many times do I feel I could *consistently* stop to give praise to the God of my understanding—eight times a day? Four times a day? Three? (Whichever it is, create your book of hours around that number—and notice whether you're able to expand the number once you've begun the habit.)

DESPACHOS

I first learned of the wonderful Andean gratitude offerings known as *despachos* after a friend returned from a trip to Machu Picchu and decided to hold a *despacho* ceremony for her birthday, on a hillside overlooking the Golden Gate Bridge, using a *despacho* made by shamans many miles away that she had brought back from her travels especially for that purpose.

A *despacho* is a bundle that, once unwrapped, contains smaller packets of symbolic ingredients, each meant to suggest a blessing for one's life. The contents of a traditional *despacho* might include alpaca fat, flower petals, quinoa seeds, and other offerings; and, as it is a spiritual ceremony, often each participant breathes their good intentions for another into a handful of coca leaves, then exchanges them as a symbol of their prayers for the other.

The *despacho* elements are meant to be seen as metaphorical, and because of that, working with *despachos* as a gratitude practice helps us to shift our focus to see the gifts that are all around us—both in the symbol and in what's being symbolized. And by noticing the spiritual messages that we can receive through such symbolic representations, we can dramatically increase our sense of inner contentment. As the Sufi proverb notes, "Abundance can be had simply by consciously receiving what already has been given."

If you would like to create a *despacho* bundle as a gratitude practice, begin to think metaphorically about the everyday items that surround you. Perhaps a coin could represent your financial needs being met, or coffee grounds could represent something in your life that was once bitter, but is now better. Popcorn kernels could represent something that has you exploding with excitement; sugar could represent the sweetness in your life.

As you begin to explore deeper meanings behind everyday objects, your world—and your gratitude—will expand. Let that experience be an invitation to start looking around at even the smallest elements of your life and reflect. What might the Divine be saying to you through them?

Inner Inquiries for Journaling and Reflection

- What do I want for my life right now? For it to be more sweet? More spicy?
- What blessings do I want to unwrap in my life? What blessings are in my life right now that have yet to be unwrapped?

> "We need to literally 'count our blessings,' give thanks for them, allow ourselves to enjoy them, and relish the experience of prosperity we already have."
>
> –SHAKTI GAWAIN

Meanings of Despacho Ingredients

Like any form of divination, the ingredients of *despachos* can be interpreted in any way that feels significant to you. Below are general interpretations for some elements commonly found in *despachos*.

ALPHABET PASTA: language, wisdom

ANIMAL CRACKERS: animal spirits

BLACK LICORICE: protection, safety

CANDY OR SUGAR: sweetness

COLORED SPRINKLES: celebration of life

CONFETTI: joy

CORN: giving back to the earth what we have been given

COTTON BALLS OR BATTING: clouds, dreams

FEATHERS: connection to Spirit, flight

FLOWERS OR FLOWER PETALS: healing

LAVENDER: harmony

LENTILS: vibrant health

PLAY MONEY: ensures the success of the *despacho*

RAISINS: elders or ancestors

RICE: abundance, fertility, fruition

SEASHELL: holds the intent of the *despacho*

STARS: connection with the heavens

SUNFLOWER SEEDS: new beginnings

YARN (MULTICOLORED): rainbow; bridge between visible and invisible worlds

"The essence of all beautiful art, all great art, is gratitude."

—FRIEDRICH NIETZSCHE

Gratitude Medicine Bags

While I was writing this book, someone from a close-knit Facebook group I belong to, someone who lives on the other side of the world and who I have never met, wrote a raw and honest post about how hard it is to hear that we are responsible for our experiences in life and that our lives are a reflection of our thoughts and beliefs, because she is going through something difficult that she did not "create" with her thoughts and beliefs—her husband's struggle with brain cancer. Because my father died of brain cancer, I have a pretty good idea of what she's dealing with on a day-to-day basis, and I empathize with her feelings. The fact is, we all sometimes face experiences in life that are so dark and painful that it can be hard to see any light—and most certainly hard to find anything to be grateful for. Yet I wrote to her in a loving response that if we can try to find something—even the tiniest things—to be grateful for when we're going through a tough time, it can soothe our swollen souls and serve as a spiritual balm that won't take away the pain of whatever it is that we're going through, but can help to soften it, make it a little less inflamed.

When my father was dying, I had a curious experience: I kept finding little charms or tokens on the ground beneath me. Once, when I was particularly distraught and grief-struck, I was getting into my car when I noticed a small flash of red—and there, below, was a flattened pin printed with the very message I most needed to feel that sad morning: *YOU ARE LOVED*. From that point on, I kept finding little things on the ground, some of which had clear meaning, some of which—like a tiny metal ship—didn't, but which kept me tethered to Source. I felt like God was speaking to me; I felt as if I were on a sort of spiritual scavenger hunt to remind me to stay present, to remember that delight is found in the most unlikely and smallest things.

Though I didn't do it then, now I would keep these little tokens in a gratitude medicine bag. Originating from shamanistic traditions, medicine bags are small pouches used to carry items for healing or reminding oneself of one's intrinsic wholeness—the things that represent the gifts one brings to the world, one's own brand of "medicine." A gratitude medicine bag could function in much the same way—holding reminders of all that is precious and sacred, that which heals us and reflects our wholeness.

It can also be a way to keep track of how we are supported even during hard, painful experiences, the times when it is the most difficult to stay grateful. Having a small medicine bag handy can be helpful to hold on to, both literally and metaphorically—by sifting through the contents of the bag, we can remember the ways in which we've been held before, *are* held by Spirit and those around us.

Whichever intention you hold as you create a gratitude medicine bag, let it support you in seeing the support that is always around you, and sometimes even beneath your feet!

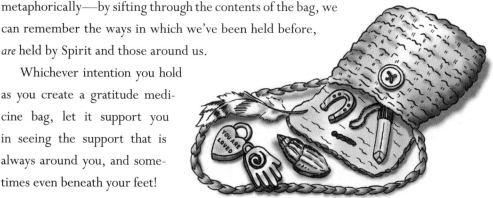

Inner Inquiries for Journaling and Reflection:

* When I've gone through dark times, what has given me comfort? For what can I always be grateful?
* How am I supported by others and by the Divine during dark times? (Pay attention to everything for clues—the newspaper someone gives you to read while you're waiting at the hospital; a brief neck rub a friend gives you as you're having tea; a shy smile from a child you see at the drugstore.)

Blessing Pillows

Every proponent of gratitude talks about the importance of waking up grateful and going to bed grateful, and of constructing spiritual practices that will enable us to bracket our days in that way. Perhaps there is no more obvious way to do that than to use our pillows, that with which we both begin and end our days, as a reminder of all that we are blessed with. As the late Irish poet and philosopher John O'Donohue suggested, "It would be lovely in the morning if you could give thanks for the gift of a new day and recognize its promise and possibility, and, at evening, it would be lovely to gather the difficulties and blessings of a lived day within a circle of prayer. It would intensify and refine your presence in the world if you came into a rhythm of framing your days with prayer."

A blessing pillow can help us to do that if we create one that reminds us to keep our days within that "circle of prayer." Depending on your artistic skill, this craft could be as intricate or as simple as you want to make it. You could decide to work with the pillow itself, or to create a beautiful pillowcase that you remove at night and put on in the morning, creating an embodied practice with which to remember your blessings. You could make a patchwork pillowcase, with each square representing a different facet of your life that you feel blessed by; or you could write a general affirmation or prayer of thanks on your pillow, using fabric pens. (One of my favorites is a chant by singer/songwriter Karen Drucker, which consists entirely of these words: "I am so blessed, I am so blessed/I am so grateful for all that I have;/I am so blessed, I am so blessed/I am so grateful; I am so blessed.")

However you decide to make and use your blessing pillow, let it indeed be a blessing—may it be a gentle reminder in your mornings and evenings to sink into the awareness, again, of how deeply you are blessed.

Inner Inquiries for Journaling and Reflection:

- In what way could I express thanks to the Divine upon awakening each morning? How might my life change if I did that consistently?
- In what way could I express thanks to the Divine upon going to bed each evening? How might my life change if I did that consistently?

"When a person doesn't have gratitude, something is missing in his or her humanity. A person can almost be defined by his or her attitude toward gratitude."

—ELIE WIESEL

Conclusion

"You say grace before meals. All right. But I say grace before the concert and the opera, and grace before the play and pantomime, and grace before I open a book, and grace before sketching, painting, swimming, fencing, boxing, walking, playing, dancing and grace before I dip the pen in the ink."

—G. K. CHESTERTON

EVERY BOOK I WORK ON, IN FACT, WORKS ON ME—I AM NEVER the same person upon completing a book that I was when I began it. This, my seventh book, challenged me in unexpected ways—perhaps because I realized with increasing awareness how vast a subject gratitude is, and how profoundly important it is for truly transforming one's life; perhaps because it gave me a lens to examine the ways in which I have been—and haven't been—living a grateful life myself.

As a Unity minister I teach the spiritual principle that the quality of our lives depends upon the quality of our thoughts and beliefs—and that we have the ability to choose those thoughts and beliefs; that we are directly responsible for creating the flavor and experience of our lives. Having explored the subject of gratitude for this book—an exploration I began many years before writing it, and certainly will continue deepening for the rest of my life—I am increasingly convinced that gratitude is the single most important key to changing our thoughts and

"Reflect upon your present blessings of which every man has plenty; not on your past misfortunes of which all men have some."

—CHARLES DICKENS

experiences. To the degree that we can make gratitude our focus, our lives will be happy and full. We will appreciate the full spectrum of people, places, and things around us—in much the same way as G. K. Chesterton expressed it in the quotation that opens this section—and our appreciation will in turn affect the quality of not only our lives, but the lives of those around us. When someone says "I'm so grateful for X," others start looking at X a little differently, start seeing it as something that maybe they should be grateful for as well. And when we can feel grateful for the entire alphabet of our lives, not just X but A through Z, too—then, well, our well-being and contentment just multiply exponentially. As Lynne Twist said in her wonderful book *The Soul of Money*, what we appreciate *appreciates*.

> "Be content with what you have;
> rejoice in the way things are.
> When you realize nothing is lacking,
> The whole world belongs to you."
>
> –LAO-TZU

I am so grateful for the opportunity to research the power of gratitude in order to write this book. I am so grateful to have had conversations with others who use their creativity in service of their spirituality by crafting gratitude practices in order to remember all that they have, every day. I am so grateful for my life, and all the elements in it—much of which is either directly acknowledged or implied in these pages. Truly, in the words of that chant by Karen Drucker that I find myself singing at different moments in my days, I am so grateful; I am so blessed—and it is the deepest desire of my heart that by reading these pages, by reflecting or journaling on the questions, and by exploring the gratitude practices that hold the most resonance for you, you will feel that all-pervading sense of gratitude and blessing, too.

Because, in the end, what we are grateful for is the Mystery, that which illumines our days with grace and delight. Gratitude practices help us to become more mindful of all the beauty that surrounds us—of the awesome privilege of life itself. Pablo Casals once said, "In music, in a flower, in a leaf, in an act of kindness . . . I see what people call God in all these things." May we, too, be grateful for the music, the flowers and leaves, the kindnesses in our lives. May we see the Holy in all these things, and in everything.

Resources

Websites

Arts and Crafts as a Spiritual Practice

Abbeyofthearts.com

Christine Valters Paintner's "monastery without walls," offering resources to nurture contemplative practice and creative expression

Artheals.org

The online resource of the Arts & Healing Network, celebrating the connection between art and healing

Braveliving.com

The portal for life-enhancing tools created by Melody Ross and family, including retreats (Brave Girls Club) and Brave Girls University (online creativity classes).

Crescendoh.com

Jenny Doh's blog, store, online classes, and other resources—because "art saves"

Explorefaith.org

A wonderful collection of articles on the spiritual life, including a "Meditate with Art" section

Janrichardson.com

The home of spiritual artist and writer Jan Richardson's various web offerings

Spiritualityandpractice.com

The motherlode of spiritual websites, featuring thousands of pages of resources gathered by Frederic and Mary Ann Brussat, including a section on gratitude

If you haven't yet joined **Pinterest.com,** you'll definitely want to sign up for a free account that will enable you to create virtual "pinboards" on every conceivable topic, including crafting and gratitude. Look for me there at www.pinterest.com/revmaggie.

Also, please join my community page on **Facebook.com:** "Creating as a Spiritual Practice."

Gratitude

Capturinggratitude.com

The "photographic happiness project" of Dr. Lauren Tober (see Nature Photographs, page 124) that has become a worldwide creativity community

Gratefulness.org

Provides "education and support for the practice of grateful living as a global ethic, inspired by the teachings of Brother David Steindl-Rast and colleagues"—and an abundance of rich material

Gratitudeclub.com

A survey, media suggestions, and other offerings from coach Caroline Adams Miller

Gratitudehabitat.com

"A place to embrace, inspire and bring to life the numerous blessings and opportunities available to each of us"—includes stories, quotations, and an online shop

Gratitudelog.com

Self-described as "the Happiest Place on the Internet"; a gratitude community that includes people to follow, ideas for showing gratitude, and ways to express gratitude with "cool, funny, and inspirational gifts"

Greatergood.berkeley.edu/expandinggratitude

A content-rich site devoted to expanding the science and practice of gratitude

Spreadinggratituderocks.com

"A global grassroots not-for-profit with the sole mission of spreading global gratitude by helping people create a habit of mindful gratitude"

Magazines

Stampington Studio publishes a large collection of magazines that may provide inspiration as you pursue crafting as a spiritual practice; a few in particular to check out are *Art Doll Quarterly, Art Journaling, Artful Blogging, HandCrafted, Life Images, Somerset Life,* and *Somerset Studio.*

Books

Creative Exercises

The Artist Inside: A Spiritual Guide to Cultivate Your Creative Self by Tom Crockett (Broadway Books, 2000)

Creating Change: The Arts as Catalyst for Spiritual Transformation edited by Keri K. Wehlander (CopperHouse, 2008)

Creativity and Divine Surprise: Finding the Place of Your Resurrection by Karla M. Kincannon (Upper Room Books, 2005)

Cultivating Your Creative Life: Exercises, Activities & Inspiration for Finding Balance, Beauty & Success as an Artist by Alena Hennessy (Quarry Books, 2012)

Making Things: A Book of Days for the Creative Spirit by Janet Carija Brandt (Martingale & Co., 2005)

Spirit Taking Form: Making a Spiritual Practice of Making Art by Nancy Azara (Red Wheel, 2002)

Spiritual Doodles & Mental Leapfrogs: A Playbook for Unleashing Spiritual Self-Expression by Katherine Q. Revoir (Red Wheel/Weiser, 2002)

Windows into the Soul: Art as Spiritual Expression by Michael Sullivan (Morehouse Publishing, 2006)

Creativity

The Artist Inside: A Spiritual Guide to Cultivating Your Creative Self by Tom Crockett (Broadway Books, 2000)

The Creative Habit: Learn It and Use It for Life by Twyla Tharp (Simon & Schuster, 2003)

Creative Is a Verb: If You're Alive, You're Creative by Patti Digh (Skirt!, 2011)

Creativity: Where the Divine and the Human Meet by Matthew Fox (Jeremy P. Tarcher/Penguin, 2004)

Freeing the Creative Spirit: Drawing on the Power of Art to Tap the Magic and Wisdom Within by Adriana Diaz (HarperSanFrancisco, 1992)

Learning by Heart: Teachings to Free the Creative Spirit by Corita Kent and Jan Steward (Bantam Books, 1992)

The Nine Muses: A Mythological Path to Creativity by Angeles Arrien (Jeremy P. Tarcher/Penguin, 2000)

Soul Fire: Accessing Your Creativity by Thomas Ryan (Skylight Paths, 2008)

The Soul of Creativity: Insights into the Creative Process edited by Tona Pearce Myers (New World Library, 1999)

Stoking the Creative Fires: 9 Ways to Rekindle Passion and Imagination by Phil Cousineau (Conari Press, 2008)

Trust the Process: An Artist's Guide to Letting Go by Shaun McNiff (Shambala, 1998)

A Year of Creativity: A Seasonal Guide to New Awareness by Brenda Mallon (Andrews McMeel Publishing, 2003)

Creativity as a Form of Spiritual Practice

The Artist's Rule: Nurturing Your Creative Soul with Monastic Wisdom by Christine Valters Paintner (Sorin Books, 2011)

Crafting Calm: Projects and Practices for Creativity and Contemplation by Maggie Oman Shannon (Viva Editions, 2013)

Eyes of the Heart: Photography as a Christian Contemplative Practice by Christine Valters Paintner (Sorin Books, 2013)

General Interest

Art and Soul: 156 Ways to Free Your Creative Spirit by Pam Grout (Andrews McMeel Publishing, 2000)

The Complete Artist's Way: Creativity as a Spiritual Practice by Julia Cameron (Jeremy P. Tarcher/Penguin, 2007)

The Creative Call: An Artist's Response to the Way of the Spirit by Janice Elsheimer (Shaw Books, 2001)

Creative Spirituality: The Way of the Artist by Robert Wuthnow (University of California Press, 2001)

Everyday Spiritual Practice: Simple Pathways for Enriching Your Life edited by Scott W. Alexander (Skinner House Books, 1999)

Illuminations: Expressions of the Personal Spiritual Experience edited by Mark L. Tompkins and Jennifer McMahon (Celestial Arts, 2006)

Simple Abundance: A Daybook of Comfort and Joy by Sarah Ban Breathnach (Warner Books, 1995)

The Way We Pray: Prayer Practices from Around the World by Maggie Oman Shannon (Conari Press, 2001)

Gratitude

Attitudes of Gratitude: How to Give and Receive Joy Every Day of Your Life (10th anniversary edition) by M.J. Ryan (Conari Press, 2009)

Blessings Gratitude Cards: 64 Ways to Be Thankful by Julia Cameron (Jeremy P. Tarcher/Penguin, 2012)

The Grateful Table: Blessings, Prayers and Graces for the Daily Meal by Brenda Knight (Viva Editions, 2013)

Gratefulness, The Heart of Prayer by David Steindl-Rast (Paulist Press, 1984)

Gratitude compiled by Dan Zadra (Compendium Incorporated, 2010)

Gratitude: Affirming the Good Things in Life by Melody Beattie (Hazelden, 1992)

The Gratitude Power Workbook: Transform Fear into Courage, Anger into Forgiveness, Isolation into Belonging by Nina Lesowitz and Mary Beth Sammons (Viva Editions, 2011)

Gratitude Prayers: Prayers, Poems, and Prose for Everyday Thankfulness by June Cotner (Andrews McNeel Publishing, 2013)

Gratitude Works! A 21-Day Program for Creating Emotional Prosperity by Robert A. Emmons (Jossey-Bass, 2013)

Living in Gratitude: A Journey That Will Change Your Life by Angeles Arrien (Sounds True, 2011)

Living Life as a Thank You: My Journal by Nina Lesowitz and Mary Beth Sammons (Viva Editions, 2012)

Living Life as a Thank You: The Transformative Power of Daily Gratitude by Nina Lesowitz and Mary Beth Sammons (Viva Editions, 2009)

The Magic by Rhonda Byrne (Atria Books, 2012)

One Thousand Gifts: A Dare to Live Fully Right Where You Are by Ann Voskamp (Zondervan, 2010)

Thanks! How Practicing Gratitude Can Make You Happier by Robert A. Emmons (Houghton Mifflin Company, 2007)

Healing/Therapeutic Applications

Art Saves: Stories, Inspiration and Prompts Sharing the Power of Art by Jenny Doh (North Light Books, 2011)

Awakening the Creative Spirit: Bringing the Arts to Spiritual Direction by Christine Valters Paintner and Betsey Beckman (Morehouse Publishing, 2010)

Craft to Heal: Soothing Your Soul with Sewing, Painting, and Other Pastimes by Nancy Monson (Hats Off Books, 2011)

The Creative Connection: Expressive Arts as Healing by Natalie Rogers (Science & Behavior Books, Inc., 1993)

Healing with the Arts: A 12-Week Program to Heal Yourself and Your Community by Michael Samuels, MD, and Mary Rockwood Lane, RN, PhD (Atria Books/Beyond Words, 2013)

Illuminations: The Healing Image by Madeline McMurray (Wingbow Press, 1988)

The Soul's Palette: Drawing on Art's Transformative Powers for Health and Well-Being by Cathy A. Malchiodi (Shambala, 2002)

Spirituality and Art Therapy: Living the Connection edited by Mimi Farrelly-Hansen (Jessica Kingsley Publishers, 2001)

Philosophy and Culture

The Art Abandonment Project: Create and Share Random Acts of Art by Michael deMeng and Andrea Matus deMeng (North Light Books, 2014)

Centering: In Pottery, Poetry, and the Person by M. C. Richards (Wesleyan University Press, 1976)

Concerning the Spiritual in Art by Wassily Kandinsky (Dover Publications, Inc., 1977)

The Courage to Create by Rollo May (Bantam Books, 1978)

Craft Activism: People, Ideas and Projects from the New Community of Handmade and How You Can Join In by Joan Tapper (Potter Craft, 2011)

The Creative Life: 7 Keys to Your Inner Genius by Eric Butterworth (Jeremy P. Tarcher/Putnam, 2001)

Desire to Inspire: Using Creative Passion to Transform the World by Christine Mason Miller (North Light Books, 2011)

Faith and Transformation: Votive Offerings and Amulets from the Alexander Girard Collection edited by Doris Francis (Museum of International Folk Art, 2007)

Image and Spirit: Finding Meaning in Visual Art by Karen Stone (Augsburg Books, 2003)

Making Is Connecting: The Social Meaning of Creativity, From DIY and Knitting to YouTube and Web 2.0 by David Gauntlett (Polity Press, 2011)

The Spirituality of Art by Lois Huey-Heck and Jim Kalnin (Northstone Publishing, 2006)

Walking on Water: Reflections on Faith and Art by Madeleine L'Engle (Harold Shaw Publishers, 1980)

A Way of Working: The Spiritual Dimension of Craft edited by D. M. Dooling (Parabola Books, 1986)

The Zen of Creativity: Cultivating Your Artistic Life by John Daido Loori (Ballantine Books, 2005)

Specific Spiritual Practices

Affirmation Decks

Inspiration Tarot: A Workbook for Understanding and Creating Your Own Tarot Deck by Gail Fairfield (Red Wheel/Weiser, 1991)

SoulCollage Evolving: An Intuitive Collage Process for Self-Discovery and Community by Seena B. Frost (Hanford Mead Publishers, 2010)

Altars

Altars and Icons: Sacred Spaces in Everyday Life by Jean McMann (Chronicle Books, 1998)

Altars: Bringing Sacred Shrines into Your Everyday Life by Denise Linn (Ballantine Wellspring, 1999)

Altars Made Easy: A Complete Guide to Creating Your Own Sacred Space by Peg Streep (HarperSanFrancisco, 1997)

A Place of Your Own by Edward Searl (Berkley Books, 1998)

Animal Totems

Animal-Speak: The Spiritual and Magical Powers of Creatures Great and Small by Ted Andrews (Llewellyn Publications, 1995)

Medicine Cards: The Discovery of Power through the Ways of Animals by Jamie Sams, David Carson, and Angela C. Werneke (St. Martin's Press, 1999)

Totems: The Transformative Power of Your Personal Animal Totem by Brad Steiger (HarperSanFrancisco, 1997)

Wildlife Folklore by Laura C. Martin (The Globe Pequot Press, 1994)

Haiku

The Haiku Box by Lonnie Hull Dupont (Journey Editions, 2001)

Haiku Mind: 108 Poems to Cultivate Awareness and Open Your Heart by Patricia Donegan (Shambhala, 2010)

Healing Haikus: A *Poetic Prescription for Surviving Cancer* (independently published, 2013;

available in both print and e-book versions at www.marjoriemilesauthor.com and www.amazon.com)

Medicine Wheels

The Four-Fold Way by Angeles Arrien (HarperSan Francisco, 1993)

Healing with the Arts: A 12-Week Program to Heal Yourself and Your Community by Michael Samuels, MD, and Mary Rockwood Lane, RN, PhD (Atria Books/Beyond Words, 2013)

Prayer Beads

Inspiritu Jewelry: Earrings, Bracelets, and Necklaces for the Mind, Body, and Spirit by Marie French (North Light Books, 2011)

A String and a Prayer: How to Make and Use Prayer Beads by Eleanor Wiley and Maggie Oman Shannon (Red Wheel/Weiser, 2002)

A String of Expression: Techniques for Transforming Art and Life into Jewelry by June Roman (North Light Books, 2010)

The Threaded Gem Adventure or How to Connect the Jewels in Your Life: Crafting Relationships Through Beads by Malana Ashlie (Tortuga Publishing, 2013; for additional resources, see the author's website, www.wisdompathway.com)

Visual Journaling

Art Journal, Art Journey: Collage and Storytelling for Honoring Your Creative Process by Nichole Rae (North Light Books, 2014)

Creative Awakenings: Envisioning the Life of Your Dreams through Art by Sheri Gaynor (North Light Books, 2009)

The Journal Junkies Workshop: Visual Ammunition for the Art Addict by Eric Scott and David Modler (North Light Books, 2010)

Journal Spilling: Mixed-Media Techniques for Free Expression by Diana Trout (North Light Books, 2009)

True Vision: Authentic Art Journaling by L. K. Ludwig (Quarry Books, 2008)

The following books focus more on visual journaling as a spiritual practice:

Art Journals and Creative Healing: Restoring the Spirit through Self-Expression by Sharon Soneff (Quarry Books, 2008)

The Artful Journal: A Spiritual Quest by Maureen Carey, Raymond Fox, and Jacqueline Penney (Watson-Guptill Publications, 2002)

Inner Journeying through Art-Journaling: Learning to See and Record Your Life as a Work of Art by Marianne Hieb (Jessica Kingsley Publishers, 2005)

Technique/How-To

Collage for the Soul: Expressing Hopes and Dreams Through Art by Holly Harrison and Paula Grasdal (Rockport Publishers, Inc., 2003)

The Knitting Sutra: Craft as a Spiritual Practice by Susan Gordon Lydon (HarperSanFrancisco, 1997)

Making Crosses: A Creative Connection to God by Ellen Morris Prewitt (Paraclete Press, 2009)
Praying in Color: Drawing a New Path to God by Sybil MacBeth (Paraclete Press, 2007)
Spirit Crafts by Cheryl Owen (CLB International, 1997)

Skylight Paths has done a wonderful job of producing books focusing on particular crafts as spiritual practices, which you could easily adapt to make your own gratitude practice. Those books include:

Beading—The Creative Spirit: Finding Your Sacred Center through the Art of Beadwork by Rev. Wendy Ellsworth (Skylight Paths, 2009)
Contemplative Crochet: A Hands-On Guide for Interlocking Faith and Craft by Cindy Crandall-Frazier (Skylight Paths, 2008)
The Knitting Way: A Guide to Spiritual Self-Discovery by Linda Skolnik and Janice Macdaniels (Skylight Paths, 2005)
The Painting Path: Embodying Spiritual Discovery through Yoga, Brush and Color by Linda Novick (Skylight Paths, 2007)
The Quilting Path: A Guide to Spiritual Discovery through Fabric, Thread and Kabbalah by Louise Silk (Skylight Paths, 2006)
The Soulwork of Clay: A Hands-on Approach to Spirituality by Marjory Zoet Bankson (Skylight Paths, 2008)

Interview Subjects

JENIFFER HUTCHINS is a painter, writer, teacher, and minister, who recently finished ministerial school at Unity Institute in Missouri. Through her artistic endeavors, Jeniffer has found gratitude in the most unlikely places. She shares the transformative power of art through her words and workshops, spreading paint—and joy—everywhere she goes. She can be reached through her website at www.jenifferhutchins.com.

VICTORIA MARINA-TOMPKINS is an intuitive, astrologer, and founding director of Flight of the Hawk Center for Contemporary Shamanism in Half Moon Bay, California. In 1994 she produced the music CD, *Flight of the Hawk: Shamanic Songs and Ritual Chants,* which continues to be distributed worldwide. Victoria has a private practice in spiritual counseling. She is a recognized leader in the fields of contemporary shamanism and spiritual mediumship. Victoria lives with her husband, John, on the Northern California coast. Flight of the Hawk offers consultations, intensive programs, and certifications in shamanism, astrology, and esoteric studies. Contact Victoria through her website, www.flightofthehawk.com.

LAUREN McLAUGHLIN is part of a team of thousands of teachers on the planet at this time whose purpose is to remind those who wish to remember that they are deeply and dearly loved by the Creator and Sustainer of All Life, that the answers to the most important questions they have are carefully stored in their own heart, and that they deliberately chose the human experience for the sheer fun of it. Lauren is a writer, speaker, and retreat facilitator who is currently living happily ever after with her husband, John, in Clearwater, Florida. Contact Lauren at her website, www.gotoelf.com.

MARJORIE MILES, DCH, MFT, author, speaker, dream expert, and creativity muse, has been featured on radio, television, and film. A former psychology professor and psychotherapist, she earned her doctorate in clinical hypnotherapy. She is also listed in *Who's Who Among America's Teachers*. Combining her love of dream work and creative self-expression, Dr. Marjorie's passion is helping people find their own voice, get their message out into the world, and "Bring Their Dreams and Muse to Life." She facilitates an expressive writing group and offers workshops, coaching sessions, writing retreats, and book festivals. For more information about Dr. Marjorie Miles, visit her website at www.journeyofyourdreams.com.

JUDY RANIERI, MA, is a legacy coach, wisdom keeper, joyologist, artist, author of *Take Time* and *Take Time for Joy,* and an explorer of life. Judy guides women to their inner wisdom, using creativity and intuition to explore the layers of knowing that we all have. Judy is a mother and grandmother, which bring her great joy and an abundance of gratitude. Contact Judy through her website at www.thewisdombox.com.

LAUREN TOBER is a clinical psychologist and yoga teacher based in Mullumbimby, Australia. She loves bringing Western and yogic psychology together in a way that is authentic, joyful, and meaningful. Lauren offers counseling, mentoring, workshops, courses, and training locally, online, and internationally. She is also the founder of Capturing Gratitude, an online photographic happiness project. Find out more about Lauren at www.laurentober.com or join the gratitude revolution at www.capturinggratitude.com.

SUZANNE STOVALL VINSON is a facilitator of the healing arts, utilizing guided meditation, visualization, and mindful creative practice as primary tools to engage both the intellect and the human spirit. She leads weekly mindfulness and creativity sessions for students at the Virginia Commonwealth University Medical Center campus as an adjunct faculty and other creativity and spirituality groups in her studio. She is an artist, creating art as a practice of self-care, and sees her art, retreats, and gatherings as creative yoga for the soul. Learn more about Suzanne at www.suzannelvinson.com and see her art at www.silvertreeart.etsy.com.

JAMIE WALTERS has more than twenty years of experience as a consultant to leaders on challenging communication issues and change, as well as studying ancestral and indigenous healing and wisdom traditions. She writes and consults for leaders and change agents who are ushering in the emergent wisdom culture. Jamie is a Berrett-Koehler author and the creatrix of the websites and online communities Wisdom's Lantern, Sophia's Children, and Ivy Sea. She lives in New York with her two fabulous felines and a stash of good tea and dark chocolate. She can be reached through her website at www.ivysea.com.

Contributors

MALANA ASHLIE is an author, holistic healer, and lover of nature. Her books and articles speak of the importance of oneness and connection, offering a new perspective to resolving old problems. She currently lives in the beach community of El Porvenir, Honduras, with her husband and pets. She travels widely, teaching workshops and retreats that incorporate ancient wisdom into modern life. For more on Malana, including contact information, visit her website at www.wisdompathway.com.

AIMEE GOLANT was voted Best Jewish Artisan Craftsperson in San Francisco in 2010 and 2011 by the readers of *J, the Jewish News Weekly*. Some of Aimee's notable artistic projects include the crown for the Women's Torah Project and mezuzot for two Space Shuttle missions and for the National Museum of American Jewish History in Philadelphia. Her art has helped raise money for such charitable organizations as Hadassah and Shalom Bayit. She founded the Metal Arts program at the San Francisco Waldorf High School in 2005, where she still teaches classical metalsmithing. She also teaches metalcraft at The Crucible in Oakland, California, and at San Francisco's Scintillant Studio. Aimee lives in San Francisco with her husband and son. Visit Aimee at her website, www.aimeegolant.com.

C. J. HAYDEN is an entrepreneurship coach and the author of four books, including the bestselling book *Get Clients Now!,* and more than four hundred articles. Since 1992, C. J. has been helping self-employed creatives, professionals, and visionaries get clients, get strategic, and get things done. C. J. also crochets, embroiders, sews, and scrapbooks every chance she gets. Learn more about C. J. and contact her through her website, www.cjhayden.com.

TESS CARLSON IMOBERSTEG is a lifelong learner and teacher of creative arts who graduated with a degree in art and theater education from the University of Wisconsin. She has worked as an instructor for creative classes in English and German in the United States and Switzerland, including classes in ceramics, wool spinning and yarn design, photography, machine embroidery, art quilting, watercolor, art journaling, and drawing. She is a Certified Zentangle Teacher and one of the founders of the Zentangle Artists Coalition; she teaches Zentangle and other classes by schedule or by request. To contact Tess, visit her website at www.tangledstringcreations.com. She can also be found on Facebook at www.facebook.com/TangledStringLLC, and has a YouTube channel, Tangled String Creations, which has examples of Zentangle drawings.

TONIA JENNY is passionate about helping others find and embrace the unique purpose of their lives. She is the spirit behind Sacred Maker—a hands-on approach to a more meaningful life. To find out more about Tonia and to contact her, see her website at www.sacredmaker.com.

AIDA MERRIWEATHER was ordained as an interfaith chaplain in 2010 after study at the Chaplaincy Institute in Berkeley, California. She has a master's degree in social work from California State University, Fresno, and worked for the Regional Center of the East Bay. She spent thirty years in children's services at her local library. She has a passion for reading, storytelling, and working with her hands, and is grateful for the chance to share her joy with others.

SØREN MASON TEMPLE says that she uses art to create the world she wants to live in. You can view her art and contact her through her Facebook page at www.facebook.com/sorenmasontemple.

Acknowledgments

HOW SWEET IT IS INDEED TO GIVE GRATITUDE TO ALL THOSE involved in contributing to this book on gratitude! First and foremost, thanks go to the extraordinary Brenda Knight, former publisher of Viva Editions, for being the "common denominator" of all seven of my books now and for her wonderful enthusiasm and support throughout the years. Thanks also to everyone on the talented team at Viva Editions; and special thanks to Jill Turney, for blessing this book with her delightful illustrations.

Heartfelt thanks to all those who I interviewed for this book and who contributed to it: Malana Ashlie, Aimee Golant, C. J. Hayden, Jeniffer Hutchins, Tess Carlson Imobersteg, Tonia Jenny, Victoria Marina-Tompkins, Lauren McLaughlin, Aida Merriweather, Marjorie Miles, Judy Ranieri, Søren Mason Temple, Lauren Tober, Suzanne Stovall Vinson, and Jamie Walters. What a delight it has been to hear your stories, and how grateful I am that our paths have crossed. And deep thanks to Melody Ross, for the blessing of her foreword.

I also want to thank my congregants, family members, and friends, by whom I feel so lovingly supported. Ongoing thanks to Janice Farrell, my spiritual director for many years, who gave me such a gift when she affirmed that I seem to have a knack for creating spiritual practices out of the ingredients of everyday life.

I am so blessed by my husband, Scott, and daughter, Chloe, in countless daily ways. Many thanks for your patience and understanding when I have another case of BMS (Book-Making Syndrome), and for allowing me the space and time to pursue meaningful projects such as this, which are so close to my heart.

And eternal gratitude to Creative Spirit for all the beautiful facets of my life . . . truly, I am so grateful; I am so blessed.

About the Author

REV. MAGGIE OMAN SHANNON, MA, IS AN ORDAINED UNITY minister, spiritual director, workshop and retreat facilitator, and author of six previous books: *Prayers for Healing; The Way We Pray: Prayer Practices from Around the World; A String and a Prayer: How to Make and Use Prayer Beads* (co-author); *One God, Shared Hope; Prayers for Hope and Comfort;* and *Crafting Calm: Projects and Practices for Creativity and Contemplation.* In 2000, Oman Shannon founded The New Story, a coaching and consulting business focused on helping people create deeper meaning in their lives.

The former editor of three national magazines, including the *Saturday Evening Post,* Oman Shannon also served as director of marketing for the Institute of Noetic Sciences. Her writing has appeared in numerous print and Internet outlets, including the *Huffington Post*, and her work has been featured in publications ranging from the *San Francisco Chronicle* to *Spirituality and Health* magazine. She has taught workshops at venues including California Pacific Medical Center's Institute for Health and Healing and Chautauqua Institution in Chautauqua, New York.

In addition to being a certified life coach, Oman Shannon completed the three-year training program of the Spiritual Direction Institute at Mercy Center in Burlingame, California. A graduate of Smith College, Oman Shannon also holds a master's degree in culture and spirituality from Holy Names University. A 2010 graduate of Manhattan's One Spirit Interfaith Seminary, she was ordained as a Unity minister in 2014.

Oman Shannon is the senior minister of Unity Spiritual Center of San Francisco, and has served as its spiritual leader since 2010. She also hosts a weekly hour-long radio show on Unity.fm called "Creative Spirit." She lives in San Francisco with her husband and teenage daughter, for whom she is very grateful.

Index